HOUSE
OF ILL
REPUTE

HOUSE OF ILL REPUTE

Reflections on War, Lies, and America's Ravaged Reputation

WILLIAM RIVERS PITT

FOREWORD BY CINDY SHEEHAN

PoliPointPress

House of Ill Repute: Reflections on War, Lies, and America's
Ravaged Reputation

© 2007 by William Rivers Pitt

This edition published in the United States of America by
PoliPointPress, P.O. Box 3008, Sausalito, CA 94966-3008
www.p3books.com

Production management: BookMatters
Book design: BookMatters
Cover design: Jeff Kenyon

LIBRARY OF CONGRESS CATALOGING IN PUBLICATION DATA

Pitt, William Rivers, 1971–
    House of ill repute : reflections on war, lies, and America's
    ravaged reputation / by William Rivers Pitt.
        p.   cm.
    ISBN-13: 978-0-9778253-2-5
        1. United States--Politics and government—2001–   2. War
    on Terrorism, 2001–   3. Iraq War, 2003–   4. Civil rights—
    United States. I. Title.
    E902.P56   2006
    973.931—dc22   2006026290

Printed in the United States of America
October 2006

Published by:
PoliPointPress, LLC
P.O. Box 3008
Sausalito, CA 94966-3008
(415) 339-4100
www.p3books.com

DISTRIBUTED BY PUBLISHERS GROUP WEST

This book is for Cindy Sheehan and her son Casey,
for everyone who has stood with them,
and for the folks in the corner of the bar.

TABLE OF CONTENTS

In the desert
I saw a creature, naked, bestial,
Who, squatting upon the ground,
Held his heart in his hands,
And ate of it.
I said: "Is it good, friend?"
"It is bitter — bitter," he answered;
"But I like it
Because it is bitter,
And because it is my heart."

STEPHEN CRANE,
"IN THE DESERT"

FOREWORD

I first encountered William Rivers Pitt shortly after my son, Casey, was killed in action in Iraq on 04 April, 2004. I would sit at my computer for hours, scouring the internet for the truth. That search led me to truthout.org, where Will was the lead writer. Like me, Will was outraged by the death toll in Iraq and frustrated that Americans weren't resisting the war more energetically. I quickly resonated with Will's beautiful writing, clarity, and passion. I could feel his emotions jump off the computer screen.

I decided to look up some of Will's earlier articles. In one from 2003, he argued that we had already lost the war against those who attacked us in September 2001. We lost that war, he wrote, because we lied to the international community about Iraq's weapons; because the liberation we promised in Iraq was as false as our justifications for the invasion; and because most of the world now saw our government as a mob of right-wing extremists with dreams of global dominance. "There is no victory here," Will wrote then. "We lost the war before the first shot was fired."

But Will didn't wait to see how the Iraq war turned out before he opposed it. Six months before the invasion, he wrote a book called *War on Iraq: What Team Bush Doesn't Want You to Know*, in which he argued that weapons of mass destruction were little more than a smokescreen for the invasion. We invaded Iraq for an ideological reason—to diminish the political power of Islam in the Middle East—combined with the prospect of huge war profits, especially for Bush's inner circle. Will tried to show this to us, but many of us wouldn't look. Having a son in the Army, I didn't want to see.

When I started reading Will's work, I didn't know we would soon meet. But in August 2005, truthout.org became one of the main news sources out of Camp Casey, which a group of us set up outside George Bush's ranch in Crawford, Texas, to protest the war. I believe Camp Casey was the jarring event that Will was looking for to energize the anti-war movement. Nine days after I sat down in the ditch by Bush's ranch, he wrote:

> The nearly 2,000 crosses, crescents, and Stars of David that make up the Arlington West cemetery, erected by the demonstrators a few days ago to represent all the fallen American soldiers in Iraq, stretch almost a mile down the country road . . . It takes a while to drive past them all. This man, who cannot abide hearing or seeing anything in the way of dissent or disagreement, saw those crosses whistle past his window. That is a victory.

At that time, Will understood something that I didn't—that an elephant must be eaten one bite at a time. Some days we can take more bites than others. Now, less than a year after the first Camp Casey, most Americans disapprove of our government's actions in Iraq, and Bush's overall approval rating has plummeted.

During that time, I've learned that Will and I have a lot in common. We both want to hold the Bush administration accountable for its lies, which flow out of the White House like beer at Oktoberfest. We're both members of the Progressive Democrats of America, and we both think the term "Progressive Democrat" should be redundant. But we haven't always agreed about everything. In March 2005, Will wrote that even though the Iraq war was wrong, he wasn't sure it was time to withdraw our troops. I quickly wrote to Will that since the war is wrong, our troops shouldn't be there fighting, dying, and killing innocent people. Then Will did something that earned my undying admiration and love; he changed his mind and wrote about it. This is one of the great things about the so-called Left. We can adapt, rethink, and reform our opinions. That isn't flip-flopping; it's being open to new ideas and fresh evidence.

For all these reasons, I was honored when Will asked me to contribute the foreword to his book. As I write it, the Bush regime is crumbling faster than a stale cookie. That disintegration is five years too late, but I'm grateful to Will and truthout.org for doing their part to expose the lies. He and his colleagues saw the scandals brewing, reported on them as they unfolded, and on some stories, provided the only reliable information. When I began speaking out last summer in Crawford, Texas, Will and truthout.org were there, and we wondered whether other Americans would raise their own voices. A few months earlier, Will had helped answer that question when he wrote, "This year, we get loud." Boy, was he right. Enjoy this book, stay loud, and grab your piece of the elephant.

Cindy Sheehan
JUNE 3, 2006

INTRODUCTION

There was a night, not so long ago, when I watched a guy get his head sawed off. His name was Nick Berg, and what he was doing in Iraq in the first place is still something of a mystery. His parents said he was over there looking for work fixing antennas that were blown up in the war, or something to that effect, and that may be true. His family is suing the federal government because at one point he was detained by the FBI, pretty much for being in Iraq. They let him go after a fashion, and he told his family he was heading home.

Somewhere along the way, however, he fell into the wrong hands. They found his dead body on a bridge in Iraq. A video of his death appeared on the internet, and the story of how he died was all the buzz on CNN and the other not-so-much-about-the-news-anymore channels. I watched the video, because that's part of what I have to do for work. There sat Berg in an orange prison jumpsuit. Over him stood five men wearing black outfits and ski masks. The one in the center read from a prepared statement in loud, droning Arabic:

> For the mothers and wives of American soldiers, we tell you that we offered the U.S. administration to exchange this hostage with some of the detainees in Abu Ghraib and they refused. So we tell you that the dignity of the Muslim men and women in Abu Ghraib and others is not redeemed except by blood and souls. You will not receive anything from us but coffins after coffins, slaughtered in this way.

The man in the center finished reading his statement, and all five of them suddenly lunged at Berg. They grabbed him by the hair and pressed his skull to the floor. One of them produced a large knife, and proceeded to slowly saw Berg's head from his shoulders. Berg screamed and screamed and screamed, and then fell silent, twitching. Once his head was off, the cutter held it up for the camera. Fade to black.

A day in the life, right? I had a very large glass of scotch next to me on the desk when I watched this horror, but all the scotch in the world isn't going to get the sound of that man screaming out of my mind. He's in there now, cemented, along with about a million other memories and facts and ideas and theories and suspicions that are the moldy bread and rancid butter of my livelihood. I've been swimming in other people's blood for years now. When you write about something, you never forget it. There are a lot of things I am never going to forget, thanks to the brutal days I've decided to write about, and maybe that makes me damned.

Two years ago, I wrote my first book. It was called *The Greatest Sedition Is Silence* and it was a ball of self-righteous howling backed by a slew of solid facts. I wrote it in the months after September 11, 2001. The book was about the attack itself, the data behind that day that never gets reported by the fraud we laughingly call the "news media" here in America. The book was also about Enron, and the tax cuts, and the Patriot Act, and George W. Bush's incredibly fake Christianity, and the need to rise up against everything that has so clearly gone haywire in this country.

I finished it at 3:00 a.m. one morning in July 2002 on the front porch of my mother's little log cabin in New Hampshire by the light of a lantern I found in the closet. It was passable for a first try, but after a thousand radio interviews and ten dozen public appearances, I learned something important: Make the book titles easy to remember. If I had a nickel for every time some talk show host or TV personality or event MC said, "And here now is William Rivers Pitt, author of 'Silence Is the Sedition Which Is the Greatest'" or "And here now is William Rivers Pitt, author of 'Sedition Is the Greatest Silence of Sedition'" or some permutation of same, I'd have a whole lot of nickels.

So I finished the book, and I printed it out, and I put it in a box, and I mailed it to my publisher, and I basked in the satisfying glow of having added something, no matter how small, to the pile. Not four days later—23 July to be exact—I got word that Scott Ritter, former head of the UNSCOM weapons inspectors in Iraq, was giving a lecture at Suffolk Law School that night. Iraq had always been a subject of interest for me, and so I hopped on the train and went down to hear what he had to say.

Room 295 of the Suffolk Law School building was filled that night to capacity with peace activists, aging Cambridge hippies, and assorted freaks. One of the organizers for the gathering, the United for Justice with Peace Coalition, handed out green pieces of paper that read, "We will not support war, no matter what reason or rhetoric is offered by politicians or the media. War in our time and in this context is indiscriminate, a war against innocents and against children." Judging from the crowd, and from the buzz in the room, that pretty much summed things up.

The contrast presented when Ritter entered the room could not have been more disparate. There at the lectern stood this tall, lantern-jawed man, every inch the twelve-year Marine Corps veteran he was, who looked and spoke just exactly like a bulldogging high school football coach. A whistle on a string around his neck would have perfected the image. "I need to say right out front," he said minutes into his speech, "I'm a card-carrying Republican in the conservative-moderate range who voted for George W. Bush for President. I'm not here with a political agenda. I'm not here to slam Republicans. I am one."

Yet this wasn't entirely true. Ritter had come to Boston with a political agenda. He was in the room that night to denounce the coming war in Iraq. According to Ritter, this coming war was about nothing more or less than domestic American politics, based upon speculation and rhetoric entirely divorced from fact. According to Ritter, that war was just over the horizon.

"The Third Marine Expeditionary Force in California is preparing to have 20,000 Marines deployed in the [Iraq] region for ground combat operations by mid-October," he said. "The Air Force used the vast majority of its precision-guided munitions blowing up caves in Afghanistan. Congress just passed emergency appropriations money and told Boeing company to accelerate their production of the GPS satellite kits that go on bombs that allow them to hit targets while the planes fly away, by September 30, 2002. Why? Because the Air Force has been told to have three air expeditionary wings ready for combat operations in Iraq.

"As a guy who was part of the first Gulf War," continued Ritter, who had served under Schwarzkopf in that conflict, "when you deploy that much military power forward—disrupting their training cycles, disrupting their operational cycles, disrupting everything, spending a lot of money—it is very difficult to pull them back without using them." According to Ritter, there was no justification in fact, national security, international law, or basic morality to justify the coming war with Iraq. In fact, when asked pointedly what the scheduling of this conflict had to do with the midterm Congressional elections that would follow a few weeks later, he replied simply, "Everything."

According to Ritter, who spent seven years in Iraq with the UNSCOM weapons inspection teams performing acidly detailed investigations into Iraq's weapons program, Iraq simply did not have weapons of mass destruction, and did not have threatening ties to international terrorism. Therefore, no premise for a war in Iraq existed. Considering the American military lives and the Iraqi civilian lives that would be spent in such an endeavor, he argued, not to mention the deadly regional destabilization that would ensue, such a baseless war must be avoided at all costs.

"The Bush administration has provided the American public with little more than rhetorically laced speculation," said Ritter. "There has been nothing in the way of substantive fact presented that makes the case that Iraq possesses these weapons or has links to international terror, that Iraq poses a threat to the United States of America worthy of war. This is not about the security of the United States," he said, pounding the lectern. "This is about domestic American politics. The national security of the United States of America has been hijacked by a handful of neo-conservatives who are using their position of authority to pursue their own ideologically driven political ambitions. The day we go to war for that reason is the day we have failed collectively as a nation."

It was almost funny. I had just mailed *The Greatest Sedition* off to my publisher. Iraq was all over the place in that book, but only one page suggested we were about to go to war there again. Now, here was Scott Ritter ringing the alarm bell about an impending invasion. I got back to my apartment, parked myself out on the back porch with my laptop, and pounded out a 4,000 word essay describing what Ritter had said. It went out the next day on the news site I wrote for, truthout.org, and was the most widely read article we published that month.

Two days later I got an email from yet another publisher, who wanted to turn my Ritter essay into another book. I reached out to Ritter, and over the course of the next two days, he and I did a long telephone interview that greatly expanded upon what he had been talking about at Suffolk. I recorded the whole thing, and in a burst of frenzied work that left me as limp as a sack of wet mice, I wrote an introductory chapter, a short history of Iraq, and transcribed my entire discussion with Ritter.

The resulting chunk of paper became my second book, a little beer-coaster of a thing titled *War on Iraq: What Team Bush Doesn't Want You to Know*. The gist was straightforward: There are no weapons of mass destruction in Iraq, no connections to Osama bin Laden or September 11, no threat to American security there, and no reason to go to war. The publisher printed 125,000 copies of the thing by the end of September 2002, and mailed a copy to every Senator before the October 10 vote to decide whether or not to back Bush's push for invasion.

Fat lot of good it did. By December it was a *New York Times* bestseller, and I became that crazy lunatic person the talk shows reached out to when they wanted someone to say outrageous things on the air: "Here now is William Rivers Pitt, author of *War on Iraq* and *Silence Is the Sedition Which Is Silent and Greatest,* who says there are no weapons of mass destruction in Iraq, which we all know is totally wrong, because of course Iraq has these weapons, because George W. Bush said so." But the war came anyway, in March 2003, and I sat on my living room floor and watched as large portions of Baghdad were reduced to their component elements in the "Shock and Awe" portion of this happy little adventure.

The days since the release of that book, since the night I watched a guy get his head sawed off, and since the deal went down in the 2004 election have been hectic to say the least. Scott Ritter, who was right in July 2002, got wrapped up in a dubious scandal involving sex with teenagers, which scrubbed him from public consciousness the following February. No proof of the scabrous allegations levied against him have ever been made public. Even if he were guilty of soliciting sex from minors, a wretched crime, he was then and is now 100% correct about the non-threat posed by Iraq.

The books I wrote carried me across more than 300,000 miles of America and Europe as I tried to spread the word, tried to rally the faithful, tried to do whatever was in my power to put a stop to what was, when you boil it down to the nub, a glaring war crime writ large. I spoke to crowds large and small. I went to Missoula and Seattle, to San Diego and Boulder, to San Francisco, Manchester, Asheville, Greensboro, Phoenix, Houston, Albany, Evansville, Kent, New York City, Indianapolis, and Lord only knows how many other cities and burgs in this country, and then I hopped on a plane to Europe in an effort to rally American expats and European allies to do whatever they could to stop the madness that had been unleashed. All in all, I hit more than a half-dozen countries in ten days during this European trip. The American side of the trek has lasted for years, and continues even now. I gave them the facts, because that is what I do. My homework is completed each night, no matter where I happen to fall asleep.

The dark side of this, of course, is what I came to know about George W. Bush, about the Iraq invasion, about the laughable "War on Terror" as a whole. A few years ago, I interviewed a man named Ray McGovern, who was a senior CIA analyst for something like 27 years. He was involved with the Soviet section of the CIA during the Reagan administration in the 1980s, and was neck-deep in the Afghanistan proxy war that was raging in that period. It is well-known that we supported the crew that became the Taliban against the Soviets during that war, because it served our Cold War purposes. We helped to manufacture the cadre of fighters that has since become known as al Qaeda, because those fighters served our Cold War purposes. McGovern said four words to me during the interview that have robbed me of many hours of sleep since: "Osama was our guy."

I have received dozens and dozens of letters and emails from the mothers, fathers, sons, daughters, wives, husbands, and friends of men and women who have died in Iraq and Afghanistan while wearing the uniform of the United States military. To a person, they denounce George W. Bush, and demand of me that I tell the tales of their fallen loved ones. These also serve to steal my sleep.

In May 2004, I was invited to speak at a gathering to commemorate the anniversary of the Kent State shootings. The night before the event, I was asked to come down to a field near where those four students died. When I got there, it was close to 11:00 p.m., and a large crowd of people had gathered. Everyone had a small candle, and had formed into a line. I was told this was an annual event, a candlelight procession around the campus to mark the occasion. I was deeply honored to have been asked to participate. I reached for a candle, but was instead ushered to the front of the line. There, I was handed a large, lovely piece of glasswork with a large candle burning within.

There were three others standing with me at the head of the line, each with the same glasswork candle. I realized, with no small dose of awe, that these four candles were meant to represent the four students who had been shot down on this ground. The candle I carried was for a young woman named Sandy Scheuer, who died at Kent State while walking from one class to another. Sandy had been a Speech Therapy student, and was not involved in the Vietnam protests that had so shaken the campus. She was walking from one class to another when the bullet laid her low, and now I was holding her light. The procession across the campus took an hour.

Though it is my job to deal in words, I will never be able to adequately describe the experience of carrying Sandy Scheuer's light for that hour, arriving finally in the place where she died. It was a parking lot, and the spot where she fell was marked by some wooden beams and a small headstone embedded in the asphalt. I stood on that spot and held her light, and raged quietly within.

All those years had passed, all those hard lessons had been so bitterly learned, all those people had died, had been maimed, had been emotionally crippled, had been destroyed, all those years had passed in this spot in a damned parking lot where an innocent had been cut down, and as I stood there holding her light, I raged because we had learned nothing. The wheel had come round; stupidity and death were the watchwords again as the country sprinted towards disaster once more in a war that served no purpose to anyone but profiteers and purveyors of hatred.

It was an honor to stand there with Sandy's light cradled in my arms, and I despised every minute of it, because all the time and hard wisdom that had passed since she fell have come to nothing.

So I watched a guy get his head sawed off. According to the man with the knife, it was retaliation for the deliberate torture, rape, and murder of Iraqis by Americans in Abu Ghraib, a prison that Saddam Hussein once used to torture Iraqis. Somehow, in a few short years, we became the moral equivalent of the Butcher of Baghdad. We invaded a country that was no threat to us, we tortured Iraqis, we raped Iraqis, we killed tens of thousands of Iraqi civilians who were no threat to us, we gave Osama bin Laden a recruiting poster for the ages, and we annihilated our reputation across the planet. We, we, we, all the way home.

The television told me that George W. Bush claimed a mandate after his so-called victory in November, and the political wizards seemed to think at the time that all bets were off. The man had a Republican House and Senate, along with a friendly majority on the Supreme Court. The unaccomplished "mission" in Iraq continued unabated; more than 2,500 American soldiers had been killed by the summer of 2006; tens of thousands more had been maimed; and tens of thousands of Iraqi civilians were dead. John Ashcroft was replaced by Alberto Gonzales, the White House lawyer who argued that the torture, rape, humiliation, and murder of prisoners in places like Abu Ghraib wasn't really torture at all; Bush used the NSA to spy on American citizens; the city of New Orleans was all but destroyed; Valerie Plame didn't have a job anymore; Jack Abramoff bought off most of DC; Duke Cunningham sold out the intelligence branches for cash and prostitutes; Osama bin Laden remained alive and free . . . the list goes on.

I have tried to do my part in all this. I wrote for truthout for more than five years, working with them to get as much of this information as far as possible into the public consciousness. I served as press secretary for Rep. Dennis Kucinich during his 2004 Presidential campaign, because what he was saying and what he stood for was an absolutely necessary part of the Democratic Presidential hoohah. I served as Editorial Director for Progressive Democrats of America, an organization of liberal Democrats, progressives, Greens, and independents that seeks to ram the purblind leadership of the Democratic Party back to its roots. I have written two books, and now a third, and maybe a million words worth of essays, speeches, press releases, fundraising letters, and campaign statements.

It hasn't been enough. When things are as outlandishly bad as they are now, "enough" isn't a word that should exist in anyone's vocabulary.

I want this book to serve as both a rallying cry and an information clearinghouse for any and all interested in salvaging what is left of our nation. The essays contained here are in no particular order, and deal with Iraq, the NSA spying scandal, the outing of a deep-cover CIA agent, the White House Iraq Group, the Office of Special Plans, fixing facts around the policy, the Abramoff scandal, the annihilation of New Orleans, the end of the separation of powers, the deliberate subversion of the Constitution, and the distinct possibility that the Bush administration may be thinking about attacking Iran. So much necessary and vital information goes by the boards in our 24-hour news cycle world. So much gets missed and forgotten. The information contained in this book is the truth of things, as best as I can deliver it, and must never be forgotten.

There must be a reckoning. It is so very much overdue.

William Rivers Pitt
Boston, Massachusetts
OI JUNE 2006

BRAIN DEAD,
MADE OF MONEY,
NO FUTURE AT ALL

17 AUGUST 2004

TO: GEORGE W. BUSH
1600 PENNSYLVANIA AVENUE NW
WASHINGTON, DC 20500

Dear George:

A really bad joke has been making the rounds lately. Some might say it's an awful joke because of the comparison. Most, however, think it's an awful joke because it isn't funny. It's too close to the truth to be funny.

The joke: What is the difference between President George W. Bush and President Ted Bundy?

The answer: Bush killed more people than Bundy.

See? I told you it was terrible. On the one hand, it is in poor taste by commonly accepted standards to compare a sitting President to a notorious serial killer. On the other hand though, the 943 dead American soldiers in Iraq, the more than 10,000 dead Iraqi civilians, the more than 5,000 dead civilians in Afghanistan, and let's not forget the large crowd of Americans you toddled off to the Texas killing bottle while Governor—all these pretty much mean you have left Mr. Bundy in the deep shade when it comes to the body count.

There are, of course, the nearly 3,000 dead people from September 11, people from all over the world. The 9/11 Commission broke out some buckets of whitewash, and like a group of dutiful Tom Sawyers, painted over the grim realities of that day. It couldn't be stopped, they said in their report. People like Richard Clarke, Sibel Edmonds, and the families of the lost who know more about the events of that day than anyone on the planet, disagree.

"Two planes hitting the twin towers did not rise to the level of Rumsfeld's leaving his office and going to the War Room? How can that be?" asked Mindy Kleinberg, a 9/11 widow who has become a leader in the truth movement. The thing is, Mindy, Mr. Rumsfeld was probably fine-tuning the Iraq invasion plan he'd been working on for years. He is, after all, a professional.

Three more American kids got killed in Iraq today, George. That makes 30 dead American soldiers in the first 16 days of August. That's 30 more names to be added to the commemorative wall that will appear somewhere in Washington DC someday. Thirty more etchings in ebony stone, 30 more people who would not now be dead but for your decisions and your actions and your appalling dishonesty.

I'm pretty bored with those commonly accepted standards that are supposed to be applied in the treatment of a sitting President. Too many people have been playing patty-cake with you over the last three years, George. Too many journalists looking to keep their sweet seat in the press crunch at the White House, too many television news anchors who think research and context is for other people, too many media outlet owners—read: "Massive corporations"—whose profit margins are intimately wed to your suicidal policies, and, frankly, too many politicians for the "loyal opposition" who have been tested in the forge of true crisis these last years, and been found to be sorely wanting.

So let's not have any patty-cake between us, George. Let's get down to brass tacks. Your people compared Senator Max Cleland to Osama bin Laden and Saddam Hussein during the 2002 midterm campaign. Cleland left two legs and an arm in Vietnam, but your people did that to him anyway. A little hard talk, East Texas style, shouldn't be anything new to you.

A wiser man once wrote this:

> Allow the President to invade a neighboring nation, whenever he shall deem it necessary to repel an invasion, and you allow him to do so, whenever he may choose to say he deems it necessary for such a purpose, and you allow him to make war at pleasure . . . If, today, he should choose to say he thinks it necessary to invade Canada, to prevent the British from invading us, how could you stop him? You may say to him, "I see no probability of the British invading us" but he will say to you, "Be silent; I can see it, if you don't."

The wiser man who wrote these words was Abraham Lincoln. Lincoln wrote this letter in 1848 while serving in the House of Representatives, years before he himself would assume the office of the Presidency. Lincoln became, in the fullness of time, a war President who inherited his war, and then pursued it with grim determination.

He summoned generals like Ulysses Grant, whose essential demeanor, in the words of Civil War historian Bruce Catton, "was that of a man who had made up his mind to drive his head through a stone wall." From March of 1864 to April of 1865, Grant used the Army of the Potomac as Lincoln's merciless fist, until white flags were raised over bloodied ground at Appomattox.

Lincoln was a war President who won his war, though the fighting of it was not his choice. He fought the enemies arrayed before him, and did not invent enemies out of whole cloth. Imagine Lincoln, faced with the Confederate insurrection, deciding to undertake an invasion of Greenland. He would have been laughed out of the White House. That's basically what you've done in Iraq.

You fancy yourself a war President, right George? "I'm a war President," you said on television not long ago. "I make decisions in the Oval Office with war on my mind." Your war in Iraq is a war of choice, not of necessity. It had nothing to do with September 11, weapons of mass destruction, or bringing democracy to the Iraqi people. It had nothing to do with defending the American people.

Your boys wanted to get paid. Cash money on the barrelhead for Halliburton, right? Almost $12 billion they've made to this point. Hey, it's good work if you can get it. All you had to do was use September 11 against your own people for months, scare them to death, denigrate the work of the weapons inspectors you agreed to send in there, flap around some claims about weapons of mass destruction (26,000 liters of anthrax, 38,000 liters of botulinum toxin, 500 tons of sarin, mustard, and VX gas, per your own words from your 2003 State of the Union address), and then fly onto an aircraft carrier and declare victory while your people were still dying.

As if that weren't bad enough, you're also losing your war of choice.

Hard to believe, isn't it? Your daddy rolled up Iraq like a windowshade when it was his turn at the big wheel. Your daddy made it look easy, which is perhaps why you thought you could take care of business over there on the cheap. Do you have trouble looking daddy in the eyes these days?

Right now, the soldiers you sent into harm's way are fighting a running battle in the holy city of Najaf, which is home to the Shrine to Ali. Ali, in case you didn't know, is considered to be the legitimate heir to Mohammed himself by followers of the Shi'ite faith. Shi'ites all around the world—millions of them in places like Iran and India and right here in America—are reacting to this action in the same way Catholic parishioners in Boston would react if someone rolled tanks on the Vatican. If you so much as chip the paint on that shrine, you're going to unite yet another group of people in explosive rage against the United States.

The gap between you and Abraham Lincoln is so wide, George, that it cannot be measured by any instruments currently known to modern science. Abe had you pegged, though, 156 years ago. You were allowed to make war at your pleasure, and the world entire is desperately wondering how you can be stopped.

You might have heard, George, about a fellow named Hugo Chavez winning the referendum on his Presidency in Venezuela. Millions of poor people flooded out of the hills to cast their votes for him, because he uses his nation's oil revenues to pay for their food and education. Quite a novel idea, yes? How many schools could we have built—schools like citadels—with the $12 billion you have thrown at Halliburton? How many hungry people in your own country could have been fed? How many jobs programs could have been funded? How many catastrophically polluted Superfund sites could have been cleaned?

That apparently wasn't on your program, George. You have eviscerated OSHA regulations—those pesky things that keep workers from getting injured and killed on the job—because you want to appear "business-friendly." The $1.5 million you got from the chemical industry in campaign funding compelled you to lower the safety standards for chemicals used in the production of super-conductors, chemicals that are believed to cause miscarriages in pregnant workers. You eliminated overtime pay for 6 million workers, going so far as to have tips for employers posted on your administration's Labor Department website that will help them screw employees out of the wages they earn. You have obliterated environmental protections across the board.

The list goes on. For a man who fashions his political persona as a "regular fella," you have delivered a large screwing to the real regular fellas who are going to have to plow through the wreckage you've left in your wake.

I worry about you, George. You live in a stark black-and-white world, and you actually think God speaks to you. There are a lot of people in padded rooms, wearing coats that button up the back, because they have had similar delusions. You see monsters every-where. Some of them do exist, to be sure, but I am forced to remember the words of Friedrich Nietzsche: "Whoever fights monsters should see to it that in the process he does not become a monster. And when you look into the abyss, the abyss also looks into you."

You have become a monster yourself, George, and the abyss is staring into your eyes. I wonder what it sees there. I know what I see.

INCOMPETENT DESIGN

27 MARCH 2006

LAST WEEK, George W. Bush got up before a gaggle of reporters and washed his hands of the mess in Iraq. The question of how long an American presence will remain in that country "will be decided by future presidents and future governments of Iraq," said Bush. To be fair, he isn't the only one. The entire administration appears to have become bored with the whole process.

Take Daniel Speckhard, for example. Speckhard is Director of the U.S. Iraq Reconstruction Management Office, which is in charge of rebuilding Iraqi infrastructure ravaged by war and depredation lo these last three years. According to a report in last week's *USA Today*, "The Iraqi government can no longer count on U.S. funds and must rely on its own revenues and other foreign aid, particularly from Persian Gulf nations. 'The Iraqi government needs to build up its capability to do its own capital budget investment,' said Speckhard."

Really. They have no police or military to speak of, the hospitals are trashed, the lights won't stay on, the flow of potable water is screwed, roads and bridges are bombed out, hundreds of buildings are wrecked, the so-called "elected" government is totally powerless to contain or control the chaos within the country, headless bodies are popping up left and right, a dozen people die every day from bombings and executions, the entire country is careening towards civil war . . . and somewhere in all this, Bush and his people expect the Iraqi government to "do its own capital budget investment."

I am going to find a china shop somewhere in the city and walk in with a free-swinging baseball bat. My goal, which will be clearly stated, will be to improve upon the place. I will spend the next three years meticulously destroying everything I see inside, from the cash registers to the display cases to the nice Royal Albert tea sets in the corner. Along the way, I will batter the brains out of any poor sod unfortunate enough to get in my way. When I am done, I will claim with as much self-righteousness as I can muster that none of the mess is my responsibility. I will then, of course, refuse to leave.

Hey, if the President can do it, it must be legal, right? Unfortunately, the difference between my china shop analogy and what the Bush administration is doing in Iraq is that I won't get anything out of it except an arrest record and a chance to enjoy my state's municipal accommodations. Bush and crew are reaping far better benefits from the mayhem they have caused.

Here's the deal, in case anyone is wondering: none of this, not one bit of it, can be or should be chalked up to "incompetence" on the part of Bush or anyone else within his administration. This was not a mishandled situation. Bush and the boys have gotten exactly, precisely what they wanted out of Iraq, and are now looking forward to fobbing it off on the next poor dupe who staggers into the Oval Office. They got what they came for, and have quit.

Consider the facts. For two elections in a row, 2002 and 2004, the GOP was able to successfully demagogue the rafters off the roof about supporting the troops and being patriotic, placing anyone who questioned the merits of the invasion squarely into the category of "traitor." Meanwhile, military contractors with umbilical ties to the administration have cashed in to the tune of hundreds of billions of dollars.

The same goes for the petroleum industries; did you know there are lines at the gas pumps today in oil-rich Iraq? It's true. The oil infrastructure is fine; indeed, it is the most well-guarded point of pressure in Iraq. There are gas lines because companies like Halliburton are not pumping the oil. They are sitting on it, keeping it as a nice little nest egg.

One would think this administration would be worried about the violence and chaos in Iraq. They aren't, because the violence has become the justification for "staying the course." Bush will mouth platitudes about bringing democracy to the region, but that is merely the billboard. What he and his friends from the Project for the New American Century wanted in the first place, and what they have now, is a permanent military presence over there. There was never any consideration of a timetable for withdrawal, because there was never any intention to withdraw. The violence today is a self-perpetuating justification, a perfect circle lubricated by blood, oil, and currency.

Keeping our attention on Iraq has allowed this administration to do what it came to do under cover of darkness. They have managed to eviscerate dozens of federal regulations designed to make sure our children aren't born with gills or seventeen eyes thanks to the pollution in the air, water, and food. The Clean Air Act is pretty much gone now, as are requirements for food safety labeling. GOP "pension reform" means growing old in America amounts to growing poor, just like in the good old days of the Depression. Millions of elderly people have been fed to the wolves by way of the new Medicare Plan D calamity. There are now tens of millions more poor people in America, the middle class is evaporating, but top incomes are up 497% according to the Federal Reserve.

The administration has also used Iraq to accomplish a goal the GOP has been pining for since 1934. Since the advent of FDR and the creation of federally funded safety nets for the neediest Americans, the Goldwater wing of the Republican party has been lusting after an opportunity to savage the government's ability to serve its citizens in this fashion. Their argument has been that it costs too much to do this, requires too much taxation, and is harmful to business interests.

This fight raged until the very end of the twentieth century. When Bill Clinton stood up during his 1998 State of the Union speech and said "Save Social Security first!" he was actually firing a directed salvo at this wing of the GOP. Look, Clinton was saying, we have trillions of dollars in the bank and the economy is going great guns. We can provide for the neediest among us without bankrupting the government or killing business. In short, he was rendering fiscal conservatives obsolete. He won the argument. Remember this, by the way, the next time someone asks you why he was attacked so viciously.

The Grover Norquist drown-the-government-in-the-bathtub crew, however, had no interest in going gently into that good night. One busted election gave them the chance to do exactly what they have done with Iraq. They have rendered it almost completely impossible for the federal government to pay for programs designed to care for the poor, the sick, the elderly, and the needy. The war, the war, we have to pay for the war, to the tune of what will be one to two trillion dollars before all is said and done. Oh, and tax cuts that go to families making more than $200,000 a year, of course.

Bush has also, in the process, managed to put himself even farther above the rule of law. Not long ago, he signed the reauthorization of the Patriot Act. Getting the document to his desk had been a laborious process for Congress; arguments and debates raged across the ideological spectrum as to exactly what kind of firewalls against executive abuse should be put into the bill to protect civil liberties.

Among these additions were a number of oversight provisions to keep the FBI from abusing their power to search homes and seize papers without notifying the resident or presenting a warrant. Other provisions required that officials within the Justice Department maintain tight scrutiny over where, when, and how the FBI put these powers to use. One new part of the bill required the administration to brief Congress now and again on these specific matters. Congress finally came to an agreement, and in March, Bush signed the Patriot Act reauthorization into law with much fanfare.

After all the worthies had left the room, however, and after all the cameras had gone, Bush quietly put his signature to a "signing state-ment" that, basically, says anything in the aforementioned law which applies to the President shall be considered null and void. The *Boston Globe* reported on 24 March that, "In the statement, Bush said that he did not consider himself bound to tell Congress how the Patriot Act powers were being used. Bush wrote: 'The executive branch shall construe the provisions . . . that call for furnishing information to entities outside the executive branch . . . in a manner consistent with the president's constitutional authority to supervise the unitary exec-utive branch and to withhold information.'"

This was the third time Bush dropped a "signing statement" into an issue of signal importance. When it was revealed that the admin-istration had bypassed the FISA laws in order to conduct surveillance on American citizens, Bush claimed his "wartime powers" gave him the ability to ignore the laws of the land. When Congress passed a law forbidding the torture of any detainee in U.S. custody, Bush issued a signing statement stating that he could bypass the law at his pleasure and torture anyone he damn well pleased.

So, to recap, the "incompetence" thing is nonsense. The Bush boys got paid; got an issue to run on in two elections; put themselves completely and totally above the law on picayune issues like torture and the unauthorized surveillance of American citizens; obliterated the central function of the federal government; and ripped up any and all regulations that would keep their corporate friends from dumping mercury into the river so as to save a few precious pennies on the dollar.

Can anyone still think this was all by accident?

The poll numbers say that nearly 70% of the country believes we are heading in the wrong direction in Iraq and here at home. This is edifying, to say the least. It means that people like me can stop try-ing to point out all the things that have gone wrong, because at last a huge majority of the country has come to see things as they actu-ally are. But it also means that we as a nation are required now to move past what is actually happening, and ask why it is happening.

Batting down the "incompetence" argument is easy; all one has to do is see what this administration and its friends have gained in the last five years. The rest of the answer is more difficult, because it has to do with us, with we the people, and the staggering degree to which we take our rights and freedoms for granted.

When we hear about our government spying on American citizens without warrants or due process of law, when we hear the President say he does not have to tell Congress anything if he doesn't want to, when we hear him claim the right to torture, all too often the response is, "Well, I'm not doing anything wrong, so I don't have to worry about it."

But we do have to worry about it. Patriots from Lexington to Gettysburg to Bastogne lie cold in their graves because they died to defend the freedoms we would so casually cast aside. Can we stand before the endless ranks of the fallen and say the rights they died to protect have no bearing on us, because we are "not doing anything wrong"? Is that not the most selfish, conceited, lazy answer we could possibly offer in the face of their sacrifice?

George W. Bush quit on us last week. He quit because he has accomplished everything he came to do. He will get away with it because, for the most part, the American people have also quit. We take what we have for granted, and assume the difficult tasks will be handled by someone else. Rest assured, they will be. They will be handled by other craven opportunists like Bush, by corporations looking to turn a profit off our indifference, by those among us who couldn't care less about you and yours.

The American people have come to see that things have gone wrong. Imagine what would happen if we decided to do something about it.

THE ETHIC
OF TOTAL OPPOSITION

03 DECEMBER 2004

I WAS SITTING at the bar the other day with Hannah, talking politics over a mug. I commented that morale among those in the progressive movement had cratered since the Presidential election, that the energy and hopefulness which had marked the long slog towards the vote had been replaced by a dimming of expectations, a hunch-shouldered feeling of despair. Hannah wasn't surprised. "I'm a cynic these days," she said. "I don't count on people much anymore."

The feeling is understandable. We've seen hundreds of thousands of people take to the streets in the Ukraine to force a showdown over a questionable election. Yet here in America, after a national election with some 30,000 reported cases of irregularities, there is this odd silence. When a former satellite of the Soviet Union shames the so-called greatest democracy in the history of the world on something as elemental as the right to vote, things are badly out of joint.

We've seen 137 American soldiers die in the month of November during the ongoing occupation of Iraq, the deadliest month to date for American forces in this war. This figure does not, of course, include Iraqi civilians, whose death tolls we never hear. Some 200,000 people were forced to flee Fallujah after Bush decided to celebrate the November election by razing much of that city to the ground in a military assault that accomplished exactly nothing. Again, we are greeted with this odd silence.

We've seen the FBI and local police forces investigate political and religious entities, such as the Quakers and the Campaign for Labor Rights, along with several peace and environmental activist groups, on the grounds that these organizations might be terrorism-related. These groups have been interviewed, investigated, and subjected to searches by a variety of terrorism task forces. It goes without saying that the groups under scrutiny are not friendly to Bush administration polices at home and abroad. The Constitutional guarantee of free speech and free association is falling by the boards, and again, we are greeted with this odd silence.

This is but a small slice of what has already happened, and cannot begin to encapsulate what may lie in wait in the coming weeks, months, and years. If the silence that surrounds everything continues, perhaps Hannah's cynicism is justified.

But then again, I met Brian Willson.

The name might not be immediately familiar to you. Willson is a member of the group Veterans for Peace, an organization made up of military veterans from every war America has fought since World War II. The mission statement on their Web page states, "Our collective experience tells us wars are easy to start and hard to stop and that those hurt are often the innocent. Thus, other means of problem solving are necessary." Veterans for Peace has been active in every demonstration against the Iraq war that I have been to in the last several years.

I met Brian Willson last summer during the VFP convention in San Francisco. Willson is a Vietnam veteran who walks on two prosthetic limbs that reach from his knees to the ground. He did not lose his legs in the war. Willson has been a peace activist for decades, and in 1987 was participating in an action to stop Naval trains from delivering cargoes of weapons to Central America. His methods were direct; he and his fellow activists would lay their bodies across the tracks and stop the trains. They had done this several times before, and each time, the trains had stopped. One day, however, the train kept going. Willson lost both legs below the knee and had a large hole blasted into his skull by the train that did not stop.

I think of everything I have sacrificed in the last four years in order to do whatever small amount I could to stop the Iraq invasion and to offset the damage being done by Bush and his people. I gave up a beloved teaching job to wage this battle full time. I have seen friends marry, have children, and move away while pursuing lives so calmly ordinary as to leave me wondering which way is up. I have let my health slide in order to concentrate on the tasks at hand. I have traveled over 300,000 miles trying to convince people that we are barreling headlong into a hard brick wall.

But I have not buried a beloved family member who was killed in Iraq while serving in our armed forces. I have not buried a family member who lived in Iraq and was killed for being in the wrong place when the cluster bombs or the napalm struck. I have not seen my job outsourced and been left to wonder how to feed my family. I have not watched my retirement fund get stolen by latter-day corporate robber barons. I did not get my legs cut from my body trying to stop a train filled with weapons from reaching its deadly destination.

If Brian Willson can wake each day, strap his metal legs to his body, and keep marching for what he believes in, who am I to despair? Considering the damage done to so many people these last four years, I've gotten off tremendously lightly. Cynicism is not an option.

There is an inauguration in Washington DC this January, or so I am told. Progressive Democrats of America is planning a summit to forge a course for the coming years. Probably you should be there. I'll be there.

Perhaps it will all come to nothing. Certainly, with Congress and the White House under the sway of people whose moral compass points ever downwards, with the highest court ripe for the molding by these people, and with a national news media that avoids hard truth the way a cat avoids water, it is difficult to imagine the break of dawn coming anytime soon. We are down to the ethic of total opposition, and as lonely as that estate may be, it is what we have, and we owe it to those who have suffered beyond our comprehension to continue as we began.

I refuse to concede defeat in any way, shape, or form. Yet I must consider the possibility that all efforts will come to naught. In doing so, I am reminded of a scene in *The Lion in Winter*. Geoffrey, John, and Richard await their executioners, and Richard demands that they face their doom with strength. Geoffrey scoffs, "You fool. As if it matters how a man falls."

Richard's reply: "When the fall is all that's left, it matters."

DONKEYS OF MASS
DESTRUCTION

24 NOVEMBER 2003

ABOUT A MONTH into the Iraq invasion, Congress set aside $79 billion in funds for the military. Recently, Bush requested another $87 billion because the occupation was dragging on far longer, and was costing more in men and materiel, than the rosy pre-war forecasts had indicated. In total, this comes to $166 billion spent on Iraq by the Bush administration.

The actual numbers, while difficult to ascertain, are certain to be significantly higher. Yale University economist William D. Nordhaus has crunched the numbers, and states that the cost of this Iraq invasion exceeds the inflation-adjusted costs of the Revolutionary War, the War of 1812, the Mexican War, the Civil War, the Spanish American War, and the Persian Gulf War combined.

Why did we do this? We did this because George W. Bush and the members of his administration argued, day after day, week after week, month after month, that Iraq was in possession of vast stores of mass destruction weapons that would be delivered to Osama bin Laden and al Qaeda for use against the United States. Some examples:

"We are greatly concerned about any possible linkup between terrorists and regimes that have or seek weapons of mass destruction . . . In the case of Saddam Hussein, we've got a dictator who

27

is clearly pursuing and already possesses some of these weapons.
A regime that hates America and everything we stand for must
never be permitted to threaten America with weapons of mass
destruction."
    —Dick Cheney, Vice President
    Detroit, Fund-Raiser, 6/20/2002

"Simply stated, there is no doubt that Saddam Hussein now has
weapons of mass destruction."
    —Dick Cheney, Vice President
    Speech to VFW National Convention, 8/26/2002

"There is already a mountain of evidence that Saddam Hussein is
gathering weapons for the purpose of using them. And adding
additional information is like adding a foot to Mount Everest."
    —Ari Fleischer, Press Secretary
    Response to Question from Press, 9/6/2002

"We don't want the smoking gun to be a mushroom cloud."
    —Condoleezza Rice, U.S. National Security Advisor
    CNN Late Edition, 9/8/2002

"Right now, Iraq is expanding and improving facilities that were
used for the production of biological weapons."
    —George W. Bush, President
    Speech to UN General Assembly, 9/12/2002

"Iraq has stockpiled biological and chemical weapons, and is rebuilding the facilities used to make more of those weapons. We
have sources that tell us that Saddam Hussein recently authorized
Iraqi field commanders to use chemical weapons—the very
weapons the dictator tells us he does not have."
    —George W. Bush, President
    Radio Address, 10/5/2002

"The Iraqi regime . . . possesses and produces chemical and biological weapons. It is seeking nuclear weapons. We know that the regime has produced thousands of tons of chemical agents, including mustard gas, sarin nerve gas, VX nerve gas.
—George W. Bush, President
Cincinnati, Ohio, Speech, 10/7/2002

"And surveillance photos reveal that the regime is rebuilding facilities that it had used to produce chemical and biological weapons."
—George W. Bush, President
Cincinnati, Ohio, Speech, 10/7/2002

"After eleven years during which we have tried containment, sanctions, inspections, even selected military action, the end result is that Saddam Hussein still has chemical and biological weapons and is increasing his capabilities to make more. And he is moving ever closer to developing a nuclear weapon."
—George W. Bush, President
Cincinnati, Ohio, Speech, 10/7/2002

"We've also discovered through intelligence that Iraq has a growing fleet of manned and unmanned aerial vehicles that could be used to disperse chemical or biological weapons across broad areas."
—George W. Bush, President
Cincinnati, Ohio, Speech, 10/7/2002

"Iraq, despite UN sanctions, maintains an aggressive program to rebuild the infrastructure for its nuclear, chemical, biological, and missile programs. In each instance, Iraq's procurement agents are actively working to obtain both weapons-specific and dual-use materials and technologies critical to their rebuilding and expansion efforts, using front companies and whatever illicit means are at hand."
—John Bolton, Undersecretary of State for Arms Control
Speech to the Hudson Institute, 11/1/2002

"We estimate that once Iraq acquires fissile material—whether from a foreign source or by securing the materials to build an indigenous fissile material capability—it could fabricate a nuclear weapon within one year. It has rebuilt its civilian chemical infrastructure and renewed production of chemical warfare agents, probably including mustard, sarin, and VX. It actively maintains all key aspects of its offensive BW [biological weapons] program."
    —John Bolton, Undersecretary of State for Arms Control
    Speech to the Hudson Institute, 11/1/2002

"Iraq could decide on any given day to provide biological or chemical weapons to a terrorist group or to individual terrorists . . . The war on terror will not be won until Iraq is completely and verifiably deprived of weapons of mass destruction."
    —Dick Cheney, Vice President
    Denver, Address to Air National Guard, 12/1/2002

"If he declares he has none, then we will know that Saddam Hussein is once again misleading the world."
    —Ari Fleischer, Press Secretary
    Press Briefing, 12/2/2002

"The president of the United States and the secretary of defense would not assert as plainly and bluntly as they have that Iraq has weapons of mass destruction if it was not true, and if they did not have a solid basis for saying it."
    —Ari Fleischer, Press Secretary
    Response to Question from Press, 12/4/2002

"We know for a fact that there are weapons there."
    —Ari Fleischer, Press Secretary
    Press Briefing, 1/9/2003

"I am absolutely convinced, based on the information that's been given to me, that the weapon of mass destruction which can kill more people than an atomic bomb—that is, biological weapons—is in the hands of the leadership of Iraq."
    —Bill Frist, Senate Majority Leader
        MSNBC Interview, 1/10/2003

"What is unique about Iraq compared to, I would argue, any other country in the world, in this juncture, is the exhaustion of diplomacy thus far, and, No. 2, this intersection of weapons of mass destruction."
    —Bill Frist, Senate Majority Leader
        NewsHour Interview, 1/22/2003

"The British government has learned that Saddam Hussein recently sought significant quantities of uranium from Africa. Our intelligence sources tell us that he has attempted to purchase high-strength aluminum tubes suitable for nuclear weapons production."
    —George W. Bush, President
        State of the Union Address, 1/28/2003

"Our intelligence officials estimate that Saddam Hussein had the materials to produce as much as 500 tons of sarin, mustard and VX nerve agent."
    —George W. Bush, President
        State of the Union Address, 1/28/2003

"We know that Saddam Hussein is determined to keep his weapons of mass destruction, is determined to make more."
    —Colin Powell, Secretary of State
        Remarks to UN Security Council, 2/5/2003

"There can be no doubt that Saddam Hussein has biological weapons and the capability to rapidly produce more, many more. And he has the ability to dispense these lethal poisons and diseases in ways that can cause massive death and destruction. If biological weapons seem too terrible to contemplate, chemical weapons are equally chilling."
   —Colin Powell, Secretary of State
   Address to the UN Security Council, 2/5/2003

"In Iraq, a dictator is building and hiding weapons that could enable him to dominate the Middle East and intimidate the civilized world—and we will not allow it."
   —George W. Bush, President
   Speech to the American Enterprise Institute, 2/26/2003

"If Iraq had disarmed itself, gotten rid of its weapons of mass destruction over the past 12 years, or over the last several months since (UN Resolution) 1441 was enacted, we would not be facing the crisis that we now have before us . . . But the suggestion that we are doing this because we want to go to every country in the Middle East and rearrange all of its pieces is not correct."
   —Colin Powell, Secretary of State
   Interview with Radio France International, 2/28/2003

"I am not eager to send young Americans into harm's way in Iraq, or to see innocent people killed or hurt in military operations. Given all of the facts and circumstances known to us, however, I am convinced that if we wait, a threat will continue to materialize in Iraq that could cause incalculable damage to world peace in general, and to the United States in particular."
   —Bill Frist, Senate Majority Leader
   Letter to Future of Freedom Foundation, 3/1/2003

"Iraq is a grave threat to this nation. It desires to acquire and use weapons of mass terror and is run by a despot with a proven record of willingness to use them. Iraq has had 12 years to comply with UN requirements for disarmament and has failed to do so. The president is right to say its time has run out."
    —Bill Frist, Senate Majority Leader
        Senate Speech, 3/7/2003

"So has the strategic decision been made to disarm Iraq of its weapons of mass destruction by the leadership in Baghdad? I think our judgment has to be clearly not."
    —Colin Powell, Secretary of State
        Remarks to UN Security Council, 3/7/2003

"Getting rid of Saddam Hussein's regime is our best inoculation. Destroying once and for all his weapons of disease and death is a vaccination for the world."
    —Bill Frist, Senate Majority Leader
        Washington Post Op-Ed, 3/16/2003

"Let's talk about the nuclear proposition for a minute. We know that based on intelligence, that [Saddam Hussein] has been very, very good at hiding these kinds of efforts. He's had years to get good at it and we know he has been absolutely devoted to trying to acquire nuclear weapons. And we believe he has, in fact, reconstituted nuclear weapons."
    —Dick Cheney, Vice President
        Meet the Press, 3/16/2003

"Intelligence gathered by this and other governments leaves no doubt that the Iraq regime continues to possess and conceal some of the most lethal weapons ever devised."
    —George W. Bush, President
        Address to the Nation, 3/17/2003

"The United States . . . is now at war so we will not ever see what terrorists could do if supplied with weapons of mass destruction by Saddam Hussein."
   —Bill Frist, Senate Majority Leader
     Senate Debate, 3/20/2003

"Well, there is no question that we have evidence and information that Iraq has weapons of mass destruction, biological and chemical particularly . . . All this will be made clear in the course of the operation, for whatever duration it takes."
   —Ari Fleischer, Press Secretary
     Press Briefing, 3/21/2003

"There is no doubt that the regime of Saddam Hussein possesses weapons of mass destruction. And . . . as this operation continues, those weapons will be identified, found, along with the people who have produced them and who guard them."
   —General Tommy Franks,
     Commander in Chief Central Command
     Press Conference, 3/22/2003

"One of our top objectives is to find and destroy the WMD. There are a number of sites."
   —Victoria Clark, Pentagon Spokeswoman
     Press Briefing, 3/22/2003

"I have no doubt we're going to find big stores of weapons of mass destruction."
   —Kenneth Adelman, Defense Policy Board member
     Washington Post, p. A27, 3/23/2003

"We know where they are. They're in the area around Tikrit and Baghdad and east, west, south and north somewhat."
   —Donald Rumsfeld, Secretary of Defense
     ABC Interview, 3/30/2003

On 1 May 2003, when he announced the end of "major combat operations," Bush proclaimed, "We've removed an ally of al Qaeda."

It is now the 24th of November. Some 9,000 American soldiers have been wounded in Iraq, according to an official Pentagon count. Well over 400 American soldiers have died. The occupation itself has almost completely bogged down. Even the "safe" areas in northern Iraq have seen a startling upsurge in violence. The two Blackhawks recently downed, killing seventeen Americans, were attacked in northern Iraq. Two soldiers had their throats cut in northern Iraq today, with a third killed by a bomb outside Baghdad.

The uranium claims were based on crudely forged documents; the mobile labs were weather balloon launching platforms sold to Iraq by the British in the 1980s; the al Qaeda claims are utterly impossible to establish as true; any connection between Iraq and September 11 was publicly denied by George W. Bush himself recently; and the mass destruction weapons are utterly and completely absent. Despite the fact that Iraq lacks any aspect of the formidable arsenal described by the Bush administration, fighters against the American occupation have managed to slay and maim our troops with sharp and deadly accuracy.

How? How are people without the vast amounts of money, weapons, and training enjoyed by American forces succeeding in killing and wounding so many of our soldiers? The answer lies in the same two ingredients that brought defeat to America on bicycles and oxen and human backs down the length of the Ho Chi Minh Trail: Ingenuity and will.

The Palestine Hotel and the Iraq Oil Ministry building came under rocket attack last week. The missiles were not fired by Iraqi men, but from the backs of donkeys that had been tied to trees near the buildings. The fuses to remotely launch these missiles were fashioned out of car batteries. The missiles struck home, gravely wounding a civilian employee of the American petroleum company Halliburton.

Halliburton had fashioned huge siege walls to protect the Palestine Hotel, an interesting fact in and of itself. One is forced to wonder exactly how a company whose purpose is to pull oil out of the ground came to be so adept at preparing military-style defenses. More interesting, though, is the fact that those defenses were defeated by donkeys. Not with anthrax, botulinum toxin, or VX gas; not with any of the 30,000 munitions Bush claims Iraq possessed; not with a nuclear bomb fashioned with material from Niger; and not with the help of Osama bin Laden and al Qaeda. Halliburton was attacked by pack mules.

Americans continue to die, the cost of this invasion continues to skyrocket, and all of the dire threats we were told of do not, in any way, exist. In short, the donkeys are kicking our ass.

HOSTILE INFORMATION

27 APRIL 2005

IN THIS SAD TIME of pre-packaged, pre-processed, corporate-controlled infotainment passing itself off as "news," it is a rare and refreshing experience to see and hear a true journalist reporting the facts. I was privileged on Monday night to share a stage in Boston with Dahr Jamail, the journalist who could not stomach the biased non-news coming out of Iraq after the invasion, and who went over there himself to see and report on what was happening.

Jamail, an unassuming spectacled man in his mid-30s, spoke in a calm and precise manner on what he had seen while in Iraq. His words carried the weight of witness, but more devastating than what he said was what he showed the crowd. For an hour, Jamail flashed photograph after photograph from Iraq on a large screen. It is one thing to hear the truth. It is another again to see it, in slide after slide, through the eyes of a man who was there and returned to tell the tale.

Jamail's photo essay described the current situation in the starkest of terms. Buildings that had been bombed out during the invasion remain today blasted and unusable piles of rubble. One photo showed a blown-out supermarket with a collapsed roof. He took the picture in 2003, but showed it on Monday night because it looks the same today as it did when the bomb first fell. There are many times many such damaged buildings. The ones that remain standing are often pockmarked from machine gun fire.

In a nation with the second largest proven stores of petroleum on earth, there are today lines at the gas pumps that make the American gas-line experience of the 1970s seem a picnic by comparison. Iraqis must spend two days in their cars, sleeping in them overnight, to get a rationed 7.5 liters of gasoline, provided the station does not run out before they get to the pump. Jamail interviewed a high-ranking member of the Petroleum Ministry, who reported that the oil infrastructure is stable enough to provide gas to the country. That gas is not being provided, said the Minister, because the Americans are not pumping it, but sitting on it.

Hospitals in Iraq are in utterly deplorable condition, with almost no medicine and few specialists to treat common illnesses and the wounds inflicted on civilians by the bomb and the bullet. Almost all the best-trained and highest-ranking medical professionals have fled the country because they are targeted by criminal gangs seeking to extort money from them, leaving undertrained Residents to handle the load. A Health Minister interviewed by Jamail said Coalition officials had promised $1 billion in medical aid. To date, almost none of that has been provided.

The sanitary conditions are almost beyond description; one photo showed a hospital bathroom that was filled from wall to wall with urine and feces, because the plumbing does not work. To make matters worse, ambulances are targeted by American forces because they fear the vehicles are being used by resistance fighters. Jamail showed a photo of one such targeted ambulance that looked as though it had been driven through a blast furnace.

In the best Iraqi neighborhoods, there is electricity available for eight hours a day. The rest of the nation gets electricity for perhaps three hours a day, if at all. At least two car bombs a day can be heard and felt, and the supposedly safe Green Zone constantly comes under bombardment. Dead and bloated cattle line the roads, said roads existing in profoundly damaged condition.

Some 70% of the population is unemployed, leaving a great deal of spare time for despair and rage to take root. A good portion of the violent resistance, reported Jamail, is being carried out by foreign fighters, Baathist holdouts, and former Iraqi military personnel. But more and more, everyday Iraqis are picking up guns, he said, because conditions are so deplorable.

The heavy-handed tactics of the American occupation force, reported Jamail, have also fed that rage. Jamail stated that the Americans have taken to using "collective punishment" against large segments of the population to try and dampen the violence. In one instance, a road leading out of a remote farm community was blown up and blocked to punish the residents, and the only nearby gas station was machine-gunned and blasted by a tank.

The most glaring example of collective punishment took place within the city of Fallujah. You will clearly recall the events of 31 March 2004, when four mercenary contractors from Blackwater were pulled from their car, butchered, burned, and hung from a bridge in that town. The American corporate news media carefully described these four repeatedly as "American civilians," failing to note that some 30,000 highly-paid military mercenaries just like these four are operating in Iraq, beyond the laws and rules of American military justice. These mercenaries stand accused by the Iraqi populace of a variety of crimes including rape and theft.

It was a despicable and horrifying act of violence, to be sure. Yet the American populace was left with the impression, reinforced by the media, that these "civilians" were targeted by the entire city of Fallujah. In fact, the act was committed by perhaps 50 people, and the Imams in the mosques spoke with one outraged voice against what was done to those four.

This did not matter. The collective punishment of Fallujah began days later. Civilians were targeted by snipers. Helicopters and bombers rained fire and steel indiscriminately on the city. After a while, a truce was called so the city could bury its dead, and so medical supplies could be brought in. No supplies made it into the city, but the casualties were entombed in soccer fields that were renamed "Martyrs' Graveyards." Jamail photographed the fields of burial mounds, and translated the names on many of the headstones. A majority of those stones bore the names of women and children.

In the lull between attacks, the citizens of Fallujah flooded the streets in a massive victory celebration, unaware that the worst was yet to come. The rage they vented on the Fallujah streets was proof enough that American tactics are manufacturing resistance fighters every day. Not long after, the second phase of the punishment of Fallujah began, this time as an aerial bombardment of the city that left thousands dead and wounded.

Bodies remained unburied in the streets to bloat in the sun and be gnawed by dogs. One Jamail photo from Fallujah showed the shattered, rotting corpse of a man lying next to his prosthetic leg. It seems this one-legged man was an enemy of freedom, a feast for dogs in the hot Iraqi sun.

The Pentagon has a phrase for the photos and reports Dahr Jamail was able to bring back to us from his time in Iraq. They call it "Hostile Information," otherwise known as unassailable facts that cut violently against the pretty portrait and non-news the American people have been spoon-fed about our occupation of that country.

If you believed the situation there was bad, it's worse than you can imagine, a war crime writ large, a grinding of a civilian population that was no threat to America and is now caught between hot steel and a cold grave. Dahr Jamail was careful in every instance to point out that the civilian leadership issuing the orders, and not the soldiers, is ultimately to blame for what is taking place. Specific soldiers committing war crimes must be punished, he said, but the ultimate responsibility for these acts belongs in Washington DC.

"Horror" is not a strong enough word to describe what Dahr Jamail showed us on Monday night, what he saw with his own eyes, and what almost no American has been allowed to see because "Hostile Information" is not permitted in George Bush's America.

WE CAUGHT THE WRONG GUY

15 DECEMBER 2003

SADDAM HUSSEIN, former employee of the American federal government, was captured near a farmhouse in Tikrit in a raid performed by other employees of the American federal government.

That sounds pretty deranged, right? Perhaps, but it is also accurate. The unifying thread binding together everyone assembled at that Tikrit farmhouse is the simple fact that all of them—the soldiers as well as Hussein—have received pay from the United States for services rendered.

It is no small irony that Hussein, the Butcher of Baghdad, the monster under your bed lo these last twelve years, was paid probably ten thousand times more during his time as an American employee than the soldiers who caught him on Saturday night. The boys in the Reagan White House were generous with your tax dollars, and Hussein was a recipient of their largesse for the better part of a decade.

If this were a Tom Clancy movie, we would be watching the dramatic capture of Hussein somewhere in the last ten minutes of the tale. The bedraggled dictator would be put on public trial for his crimes, sentenced to several thousand concurrent life sentences, and dragged off to prison in chains. The anti-American insurgents in Iraq, seeing the sudden futility of their fight to place Hussein back into power, would lay down their arms and melt back into the countryside.

For dramatic effect, more than a few would be cornered by SEAL teams in black facepaint and discreetly shot in the back of the head. The President would speak with eloquence as the martial score swelled around him. Fade to black, roll credits, get off my plane.

The real-world version is certainly not lacking in drama. Unfortunately, the real-world script has a lot of pages left to be turned. Former UN weapons inspector Scott Ritter, reached at his home on Sunday, said, "It's great that they caught him. The man was a brutal dictator who committed terrible crimes against his people. But now we come to rest of story. We didn't go to war to capture Saddam Hussein. We went to war to get rid of weapons of mass destruction. Those weapons have not been found."

Ray McGovern, senior analyst and 27-year veteran of the CIA, echoed Ritter's perspective on Sunday. "It's wonderful that he was captured, because now we'll find out where the weapons of mass destruction are," said McGovern with tongue firmly planted in cheek. "We killed his sons before they could tell us."

When they found Hussein hiding in that dirt hole in the ground, none of this stuff was down there with him. The full force of the American military has been likewise unable to locate it anywhere else. There is no evidence of al Qaeda agents working with Hussein, and Bush was forced some weeks ago to publicly acknowledge that Hussein had nothing to do with September 11. The Niger uranium story was debunked last summer.

Conventional wisdom now holds that none of this stuff was there to begin with. So all the clear statements from virtually everyone in the Bush administration squatting on the public record describing the existence of this stuff look now like what they were then: A lot of overblown rhetoric and outright lies, designed to terrify the American people into supporting an unnecessary go-it-alone war. Said war made a few Bush cronies rich beyond the dreams of avarice, while allowing some hawks in the Defense Department to play at empire-building, something they have been craving for more than ten years.

Of course, the rhetoric mutated as the weapons stubbornly refused to be found. By the time Bush did his little "Mission Accomplished" strut across the aircraft carrier, the occupation was about the removal of Saddam Hussein and the liberation of the Iraqi people. No longer were we informed on a daily basis of the "sinister nexus between Hussein and al Qaeda," as described by Colin Powell before the United Nations in February. No longer were we fed the insinuations that Hussein was involved in the attacks of September 11. Certainly, any and all mention of weapons of mass destruction ceased completely. We were, instead, embarking on some noble democratic experiment.

The capture of Saddam Hussein feeds nicely into these newly minted explanations. Mr. Bush and his people will use this as the propaganda coup it is, and to great effect. But a poet once said something about tomorrow, and tomorrow, and tomorrow.

"We are not fighting for Saddam," said an Iraqi "insurgent" named Kashid Ahmad Saleh in a *New York Times* report from a week ago. "We are fighting for freedom and because the Americans are Jews. The Governing Council is a bunch of looters and criminals and mercenaries. We cannot expect that stability in this country will ever come from them."

"The principle is based on religion and tribal loyalties," continued Saleh. "The religious principle is that we cannot accept to live with infidels. The Prophet Muhammad, peace be on him, said, `Hit the infidels wherever you find them.' We are also a tribal people. We cannot allow strangers to rule over us."

Welcome to the new Iraq. The theme that the 455 Americans killed there, and the thousands of others who have been wounded, fell at the hands of pro-Hussein loyalists is now gone. The Bush administration's celebrations over this capture will appear quite silly and premature when the dying continues. Whatever Hussein bitter-enders there are will be joined by Iraqi nationalists who will now see no good reason for American forces to remain. After all, the new rhetoric highlighted the removal of Hussein as the reason for this invasion, and that task has been completed. Yet American forces are not leaving, and will not leave. The killing of our troops will continue because of people like Kashid Ahmad Saleh. All Hussein's capture did for Saleh was remove from the table the idea that he was fighting for the dictator. He is free now, and the war will begin in earnest.

The dying will continue because America's presence in Iraq is a wonderful opportunity for a man named Osama bin Laden, who was not captured on Saturday. Bin Laden, it has been reported, is thrilled by what is happening in Iraq, and plans to throw as much violence as he can muster at American forces there. The Bush administration spent hundreds of billions of dollars on this Iraq invasion, not one dime of which went towards the capture or death of the fellow who, we are told, brought down the Towers a couple of years ago. For bin Laden and his devotees, Iraq is better than Disneyland.

For all the pomp and circumstance that has surrounded the extraction of the former Iraqi dictator from a hole in the ground, the reality is that the United States is not one bit safer now that the man is in chains. There will be no real trial for Hussein, because he might start shouting about the back pay he is owed from his days as an employee of the American government. And because another former employee of the American government is still alive and free in the Tora Bora caves, our troops are still in mortal danger in Iraq.

Hussein was never a threat to the United States. His capture means nothing to the safety and security of the American people. The money we spent to put the bag on him might have gone towards capturing bin Laden, but that did not happen. A free bin Laden serves the Bush administration; he is their Emmanuel Goldstein, their Two Minutes Hate, their ace in the hole. We can be happy for the people of Iraq, because their Hussein problem is over. Here in America, our Hussein problem is just beginning. The other problem, that Osama fellow we should have been trying to capture this whole time, remains perched over our door like the raven.

WINNEBAGOS OF DEATH

I'VE BEEN DIGGING into one of the justifications for invading Iraq proffered by the Bush crew over the last two years. Bear with me, as this gets into chemistry.

Let's take a look at the Winnebagos of Death. You will remember these as the mobile biological weapons laboratories in Iraq so dramatically described by Colin Powell before the UN in February of 2003. "We have firsthand descriptions," said Powell, "of biological weapons factories on wheels and on rails. The trucks and train cars are easily moved and are designed to evade detection by inspectors. In a matter of months, they can produce a quantity of biological poison equal to the entire amount that Iraq claimed to have produced in the years prior to the Gulf War. Ladies and gentlemen, these are sophisticated facilities. For example, they can produce anthrax and botulism toxin."

Scary stuff. Too bad it wasn't true.

The basis for these claims came from a CIA/DIA report that was made public in May of 2003. Since its release, and Powell's performance before the UN, the report has been shot to pieces.

In June of 2003, the UK *Guardian* reported, "An official British investigation into two trailers found in northern Iraq has concluded they are not mobile germ warfare labs, as was claimed by Tony Blair and President George Bush, but were for the production of hydrogen

45

to fill artillery balloons, as the Iraqis have continued to insist. The revelation that the mobile labs were to produce hydrogen for artillery balloons will also cause discomfort for the British authorities because the Iraqi army's original system was sold to it by the British company, Marconi Command & Control."

The thing is, despite the fact that Powell publicly distanced himself from his now-humiliating UN display, and despite several reports in the British press describing in detail what these mobile facilities were actually used for, you can still hear Bush defenders talk about them in the American press to defend the invasion. The story behind the CIA/DIA report and its massive flaws has not been widely reported over here. Yet it was one of several key threats thrown at the American people to justify a war.

"They can produce enough dry biological agent in a single month," said Powell in February of 2003, "to kill thousands upon thousands of people. And dry agent of this type is the most lethal form for human beings." In other words, bring me the plastic sheeting and duct tape, because we're all going to die.

I spoke at length with Brad Spencer, PhD, an expert in this area, who took a great deal of time to explain the flaws in the CIA/DIA report, and the flaws in the subsequent scaremongering that came out of the White House.

"Bush was relying on the CIA/DIA white paper that purported to conclude that the trailers found in Iraq were mobile biological culture systems," said Spencer. "That's the only apparent 'hard' evidence he ever cited, and it was false from the start. There are obvious fabrications in the white paper, fabrications that fly in the face of science. It's garbage. It's a lie. It is the most easily proved of all the lies yet it is still allowed to stand. I have made hydrogen using the same reaction as was used by the Iraqis on those trailers. I could and did determine, from the information in the white paper itself, that the trailers were for hydrogen manufacture. How much more blatant and obvious do you need a lie to be before you expose it as such?"

As I have never been an ace in the science department, I asked Dr.

Spencer to describe in detail the problems with the report. "To start with," he said, "I've known since the 1970s, when I was in graduate school, that the reaction used on the trailers generates a lot of heat along with the hydrogen and that the cooling unit is a necessary part of the system. Anybody that runs the reaction will discover that fact. The fable the white paper weaves about the Iraqis discovering that the heat of summer interfered with WMD culture and adding the unit (the white paper says it was added 'because the drawings by Powell showed no cooling unit and the difference had to be explained') is utter nonsense.

"In reality," said Spencer, "any competently designed biological culture system, mobile or otherwise, would have to have not merely a cooling unit but a full temperature control system for the culture vessel. That was utterly lacking in the drawings shown by Powell at the UN and apparently utterly lacking in the expensive mock-up of such trailers constructed by the U.S. (David Kay was on that team) before the war. That it is only a cooling unit and not a temperature control system is actually strong evidence that the trailers are not for biological WMD culture—exactly opposite to the white paper claim but in accord with the requirements of both kinds of system.

"The reaction used on the trailer to make hydrogen (aluminum metal plus sodium hydroxide plus water)," said Spencer, "has been used for that purpose since at least the early part of the 20th century (there's at least one U.S. patent from that date for a system that uses that reaction) and was also mentioned in a 1960s or 1970s *National Geographic* article, which is where I learned of it. I was in graduate school at the time and tried the reaction at home, learning in the process that the heat was produced: I ended up more than once with a bottle of boiling lye solution with a balloon on the neck of the bottle. The trailers would surely have to produce hydrogen at something like 100 to 1000 times the volume I produced, with corresponding increase in the amount of heat evolved. It would be essential to remove that heat to avoid damage to valves and pumps from boiling lye.

"The culture vessel also would not be the very obvious pressure vessel seen in the photograph in the white paper," Spencer continued. "The trailer had no shocks, no springs. It would be idiotic to do a biological culture under pressure on such a system: The stresses involved in moving the trailer would cause leaks and a biological WMD culture system under pressure would spew biological WMD out from any leak. Nor is there likely to be an advantage to doing the culture under pressure: Pressure is used to enhance the yields of chemical reactions in the gas phase where the reactant gases combine to form a product gas. When the number of molecules of product gas is less than the number of molecules of reactant gas, for example in the manufacture of polyethylene, increased pressure does increase yield.

"The compressor and gas bottles are needed to compress and store the hydrogen," said Spencer, "as the white paper essentially admits. The fable about a tell-tale off-gas that had to be compressed and stored is fantastically ridiculous. The UN inspectors weren't monitoring the atmosphere for any such by-product, the white paper identifies no such by-product, biological WMD, or biological WMD culture process. If there were a tell-tale gaseous by-product, simple combustion would destroy it, just as drawing crankcase vapors into the intake manifold of a car destroys those vapors. It isn't biological WMD processes that create indestructible tell-tale by-products, it's nuclear ones. It's a fable spun by a non-technical person whose main skill appears to be twisting facts to fit a story. There's not a shred of evidence that the compressor was for the purpose of capturing any by-product: it's a story from the imagination of someone with low technical skills—a person of greater skill would recognize how fantastic the story is.

"The white paper claims that the fact the trailers had recently been repainted was evidence of efforts to conceal use of the trailers for WMD culture," said Spencer. "If there was such evidence, the paint would cover and preserve the evidence. Scratch it off and do an analysis. That, too, is glossed over. It's a cooked story, created by a non-technical person. It's indefensible. There's literally no hard evidence to back up the claim that the trailers were for WMD culture, no evidence for the cooling unit fable, no evidence for the compressor and gas bottle fable.

"Not only did the CIA issue a very unusual report to the people, something very rare for the CIA to do," concluded Spencer, "the report contains completely unsupported claims. Who can possibly maintain that the CIA did that on their own, with no pressure applied? Who can believe that, unprodded, the CIA decided to issue a white paper containing wild speculations? When the CIA subsequently produced the Duelfer report all such fantasies disappeared, and the Duelfer report correctly concluded that the trailers were for hydrogen production. It's the same CIA, the same analysts, nearly the same evidence. Something made them behave strangely in 2003, right when the administration was desperate for some proof of Iraqi WMD activity. It's also worth noting who it was in the administration that relied on the white paper the longest, continuing to do so even after it was revealed that 'Curveball' was an unreliable source and after Colin Powell had disavowed his own UN presentation."

I got a funny email the other day that covers a similar situation. The email observed something amusing about Ibn al-Shaykh al-Libi, the so-called "source" who claimed that Iraq was hosting al Qaeda terrorists. His information was used by Bush, Cheney, Rumsfeld, Rice, Powell, and the rest of them to justify the invasion, even though the Defense Intelligence Agency warned them that al-Libi was lying through his teeth. It turns out, in fact, that al-Libi was indeed crafting extravagant lies about al Qaeda in Iraq out of whole cloth, and eventually recanted all of his testimony in 2004.

So here's the funny part: If you sound out the name Ibn al-Shaykh al-Libi in just the right way, it sounds an awful lot like "I've been a shaky alibi." Indeed, he was. It seems we can lump Mr. Shaky Alibi in with this report on the Winnebagos of Death. You've got to love serendipity.

THE DOG ATE MY WMD

13 JUNE 2003

AFTER SEVERAL YEARS teaching high school, I've heard all the excuses. I didn't get my homework done because my computer crashed, because my project partner didn't do their part, because I feel sick, because I left it on the bus, because I had a dance recital, because I was abducted by aliens and viciously probed. Houdini doesn't have as many tricks. No one on earth is more inventive than a high school sophomore backed into a corner and faced with a zero on an assignment.

No one, perhaps, except Bush administration officials forced now to account for their astounding claims made since September 2002 regarding Iraq's alleged weapons program.

There have been roughly 280 days' worth of fearful descriptions of the formidable Iraqi arsenal, coming on the heels of seven years of UNSCOM weapons inspections, four years of surveillance, and months of UNMOVIC weapons inspections. Add to that the occupation of an entire nation by American and British forces, after which said forces searched "everywhere" per the words of the Marine commander over there and "found nothing;" the interrogation of dozens of the scientists and officers who have nothing to hide anymore because Hussein is gone; and the discovery that the dreaded "mobile labs" were weather balloon platforms sold to Iraq by the British. George W. Bush and his people suddenly have a few things to answer for.

You may recall the following bombastic claim made by Mr. Bush during his constitutionally mandated State of the Union address on 28 January 2003: "Our intelligence officials estimate that Saddam Hussein had the materials to produce as much as 500 tons of sarin, mustard and VX nerve agent." Nearly five months later, those 500 tons are nowhere to be found. A few seconds with a calculator can help us understand exactly what this means.

Five hundred tons of gas equals 1 million pounds. After UNSCOM, after UNMOVIC, after the war, after the U.S. Army inspectors, after all the satellite surveillance, it is extremely difficult to imagine how 1 million pounds of anything could refuse to be located. Bear in mind, also, that this 1 million pounds is but a part of the Iraqi weapons arsenal described by Bush and his administration.

Maybe the dog ate it. Or maybe it was never there to begin with, having been destroyed years ago by the first UN inspectors and by the Iraqis themselves. Maybe we went to war on a big lie, one that killed over 3,500 Iraqi civilians to date, one that killed some 170 American soldiers, one that has been costing us one American soldier's life per day thus far.

If you listen to the Republicans on Capitol Hill, however, this is all just about "politics." An in-depth investigation into how exactly we went to war on the WMD word of the Bush administration has been quashed by the Republican majority in the House of Representatives. Closed-door hearings by the Intelligence Committee are planned next week, but an open investigation has been shunted aside by Bush allies who control the gavel and the agenda. If there is nothing to hide, as the administration insists, if nothing was done wrong, one must wonder why they fear to have these questions asked in public.

The questions are being asked anyway. Thirty-five Representatives have signed House Resolution 260, which demands with specificity that the administration back up it's oft-repeated claims about the

Iraqi weapons arsenal with evidence and fact. The guts of the Resolution are as follows:

> Resolved, That the President is requested to transmit to the House of Representatives not later than 4 days after the date of the adoption of this resolution documents or other materials in the President's possession that provide specific evidence for the following claims relating to Iraq's weapons of mass destruction:
>
> (1) On August 26, 2002, the Vice President in a speech stated: "Simply stated, there is no doubt that Saddam Hussein now has weapons of mass destruction . . . What he wants is time, and more time to husband his resources to invest in his ongoing chemical and biological weapons program, and to gain possession of nuclear weapons."
>
> (2) On September 12, 2002, in a speech to the United Nations General Assembly, the President stated: "Right now, Iraq is expanding and improving facilities that were used for the production of biological weapons . . . Iraq has made several attempts to buy high-strength aluminum tubes used to enrich uranium for a nuclear weapon."
>
> (3) On October 7, 2002, in a speech in Cincinnati, Ohio, the President stated: "It possesses and produces chemical and biological weapons. It is seeking nuclear weapons . . . And surveillance photos reveal that the regime is rebuilding facilities that it had used to produce chemical and biological weapons."
>
> (4) On January 7, 2003, the Secretary of Defense at a press briefing stated: "There is no doubt in my mind but that they currently have chemical and biological weapons."
>
> (5) On January 9, 2003, in his daily press briefing, the White House spokesperson stated: "We know for a fact that there are weapons in Iraq."
>
> (6) On March 16, 2003, in an appearance on NBC's "Meet the Press," the Vice President stated: "We believe he has, in fact, reconstituted nuclear weapons. I think Mr. El Baradei frankly is wrong."
>
> (7) On March 17, 2003, in an Address to the Nation, the President stated: "Intelligence gathered by this and other governments leaves no doubt that the Iraq regime continues to possess and conceal some of the most lethal weapons ever devised."
>
> (8) On March 21, 2003, in his daily press briefing, the White House spokesperson stated: "Well, there is no question that we

have evidence and information that Iraq has weapons of mass destruction, biological and chemical particularly . . . All this will be made clear in the course of the operation, for whatever duration it takes."

(9) On March 24, 2003, in an appearance on CBS's "Face the Nation," the Secretary of Defense stated: "We have seen intelligence over many months that they have chemical and biological weapons, and that they have dispersed them and that they're weaponized and that, in one case at least, the command and control arrangements have been established."

(10) On March 30, 2003, in an appearance on ABC's "This Week," the Secretary of Defense stated: "We know where they are, they are in the area around Tikrit and Baghdad."

On 10 June 2003, Representative Henry Waxman transmitted a letter to Condoleezza Rice demanding answers to a specific area of concern in this whole mess. His letter goes on to repeat, in scathing detail, the multifaceted claims made by the Bush administration regarding an Iraqi nuclear weapons program, and deconstructs those claims with a fine scalpel. "What I want to know is the answer to a simple question: Why did the President use forged evidence in the State of the Union address?" the letter concludes. "This is a question that bears directly on the credibility of the United States, and it should be answered in a prompt and forthright manner, with full disclosure of all the relevant facts."

It is this aspect, the nuclear claims, that has led the Bush administration to do what many observers expected them to do for a while now: They have blamed it all on the CIA. A report in the 12 June 2002 edition of the *Washington Post* cites an unnamed Bush administration official who claims that the CIA knew the evidence of Iraqi nuclear plans had been forged, but that the CIA failed to give this information to Bush. The *Post* story states, "A senior intelligence official said the CIA's action was the result of 'extremely sloppy' handling of a central piece of evidence in the administration's case against then-Iraqi President Saddam Hussein."

Ergo, it wasn't the dog who ate the WMDs. It was the CIA.

Unfortunately for Bush and his people, this blame game will not hold water.

Early in October of 2002, Bush went before the American people and delivered yet another vat of nightmarish descriptions of what Saddam Hussein could do to America and the world with his vast array of weaponry. One week before this speech, however, the CIA had publicly stated that Hussein and Iraq were less of a threat than they had been for the last ten years.

Columnist Robert Scheer reported on 9 October 2002, that, "In its report, the CIA concludes that years of UN inspections combined with U.S. and British bombing of selected targets have left Iraq far weaker militarily than in the 1980s, when it was supported in its war against Iran by the United States. The CIA report also concedes that the agency has no evidence that Iraq possesses nuclear weapons."

Certainly, if citizen Scheer was able to read and understand the CIA report on Iraq's nuclear capabilities, the President of the United States should have been able to do so as well.

The scandal that laid Bill Clinton low centered around his lying under oath about sex. The scandal which took down Richard Nixon was certainly more profound, as he was accused of misusing the CIA and FBI to spy on political opponents while paying off people to lie about his actions. Lying under oath and misusing the intelligence community are both serious transgressions, to be sure. The matter of Iraq's weapons program, however, leaves both of these in deep shade.

George W. Bush and his people used the fear and terror that still roils within the American people in the aftermath of September 11 to fob off an unnerving fiction about a faraway nation, and then used that fiction to justify a war that killed thousands and thousands of people. Latter-day justifications about "liberating" the Iraqi people or demonstrating the strength of America to the world do not obscure this fact. They lied us into a war that, beyond the death toll, has served as the greatest al Qaeda recruiting drive in the history of the world. They lied about a war that cost billions of dollars which could have been better used to bolster America's amazingly substandard anti-terror defenses. They are attempting, in the aftermath, to misuse the CIA by blaming them for all of it.

Blaming the CIA will not solve this problem, for the CIA is well able to defend itself. Quashing investigations in the House will not stem the questions that come now at a fast and furious clip.

They lied. Period. Trust a teacher on this. We can spot liars who have not done their homework a mile away.

THE HEART OF THE MATTER

17 OCTOBER 2005

As to U.S. assertions that Iraq possessed bombs, rockets and shells for poison agents, unmanned aerial vehicles for delivering biological and chemical weapons, nuclear weapon materials, sarin, tabun, mustard agent, precursor chemicals, VX nerve agent, anthrax, aflotoxins, ricin and surface-to-surface Al Hussein missiles, not one has so far been found. One vial of Strain B Botulinum toxin is found in the domestic refrigerator of an Iraqi scientist. It is ten years old. Hans Blix comments, "They wanted to come to the conclusion that there were weapons. Like the former days of the witch hunt, they are convinced that they exist. And if you see a black cat, well, that's evidence of the witch."

—*Stuff Happens*, a play by David Hare

IN A *New York Times* ARTICLE published on Sunday, columnist Frank Rich buried the dart right in the center-black. "What matters most in this case," wrote Rich, "is not whether Mr. Rove and Lewis Libby engaged in a petty conspiracy to seek revenge on a whistle-blower, Joseph Wilson, by unmasking his wife, Valerie, a covert C.I.A. officer. What makes Patrick Fitzgerald's investigation compelling, whatever its outcome, is its illumination of a conspiracy that was not at all petty: the one that took us on false premises into a reckless and wasteful war in Iraq. That conspiracy was instigated by Mr. Rove's boss, George W. Bush, and Mr. Libby's boss, Dick Cheney."

That last sentence strikes sparks, for it takes us beyond the minutiae of a case surrounding two senior White House aides. However important Rove and Libby may be to this administration, neither represents the end of the story. George W. Bush and Dick Cheney, with deliberation and intent, took this country to war in Iraq based on false premises, inflated intelligence, and bald-faced scare tactics. They used September 11 against their own people to get what they wanted. That is the heart of this matter. If Fitzgerald's investigation ends at Rove and Libby, it will have ended too soon.

Rich, in his article, details the existence of the White House Iraq Group, or WHIG. "Its inception in August 2002, seven months before the invasion of Iraq," wrote Rich, "was never announced. Its eight members included Mr. Rove, Mr. Libby, Condoleezza Rice and the spinmeisters Karen Hughes and Mary Matalin. Its mission: to market a war in Iraq. Of course, the official Bush history would have us believe that in August 2002 no decision had yet been made on that war. Dates bracketing the formation of WHIG tell us otherwise. On July 23, 2002 — a week or two before WHIG first convened in earnest — a British official told his peers, as recorded in the now famous Downing Street memo, that the Bush administration was ensuring that 'the intelligence and facts' about Iraq's W.M.D.'s 'were being fixed around the policy' of going to war."

WHIG, and its intention to sell an unnecessary war to a shell-shocked public, is only half the story. The other half of the manipulative sales team could be found in the neighborhood occupied by the Department of Defense. The Office of Special Plans, or OSP, was created by Defense Secretary Donald Rumsfeld specifically to second-guess and reinterpret intelligence data to justify war in Iraq. Think of it like baseball: the OSP pitched, and WHIG caught.

The OSP was on no government payroll and suffered no congressional oversight. Their tainted information and interpretations overtopped the Iraq data being provided by the State Department and CIA. The OSP was able to accomplish this thanks to devoted patronage from high-ranking members of the administration, most prominently Vice President Cheney.

The highest levels of the OSP were staffed by heavy-hitters like Undersecretary of Defense for Policy Douglas J. Feith and William Luti, a former Navy officer who worked for Cheney before joining the Pentagon. When the OSP wanted to intimidate analysts into shaping conclusions to fit the already-made war decision, Cheney went to CIA headquarters on unprecedented visits. Once there, he demanded "forward-leaning" interpretations of the evidence. When Cheney was unable to go to the CIA, his chief of staff, Lewis "Scooter" Libby, went in his place.

That's it, right there. Mr. Libby may be a target of Mr. Fitzgerald, but no one should forget the trips Cheney personally made to Langley in order to wring war-supporting evidence out of the analysts. He went himself. His fingerprints are all over this.

One name that has been lost in the shuffle of history is that of Air Force Lt. Col. Karen Kwiatkowski, who worked in the office of Under Secretary of Defense for Policy Douglas Feith until her retirement. Kwiatkowski charged two years ago that the operations she witnessed during her tenure in Feith's office, and particularly those of the OSP, constituted "a subversion of constitutional limits on executive power and a co-optation through deceit of a large segment of the Congress."

"What I saw was aberrant, pervasive and contrary to good order and discipline," Kwiatkowski wrote after her retirement. "If one is seeking the answers to why peculiar bits of 'intelligence' found sanctity in a presidential speech, or why the post-Saddam occupation has been distinguished by confusion and false steps, one need look no further than the process inside the Office of the Secretary of Defense."

According to Kwiatkowsky, the political appointees assigned there and their contacts at State, the NSC, and Cheney's office tended to work as a "network." Feith's office often deliberately cut out, ignored, or circumvented normal channels of communication both within the Pentagon and with other agencies. "I personally witnessed several cases of staff officers being told not to contact their counterparts at

State or the NSC because that particular decision would be processed through a different channel," wrote Kwiatkowsky.

That "different channel," we now know, was almost certainly WHIG.

Ambassador Joseph Wilson's public repudiation of Bush for using the now-rubbished Niger uranium evidence, and his attack upon the entire rationale for invasion, was a direct and ominous threat to the latticework of disinformation and lies put forth by WHIG and OSP. They didn't attack Wilson's wife because they didn't like her, or because they were bored. They did it because Wilson could have almost single-handedly dismantled the administration's case for war. They did it to warn any other insiders who might have wanted to talk that there would be serious consequences for public statements. The administration's case for war was championed not by Rove and Libby, but by Bush and Cheney. It was their party, and Wilson was looking to stop the music.

Two questions remain: why would the administration take such a fantastic risk in attacking Wilson, and where are Bush's fingerprints on this thing? Both questions can be answered by another tidbit that has fallen down the memory hole. On 22 May 2003, two months after the invasion of Iraq, George W. Bush signed an Executive Order titled "Protecting the Development Fund for Iraq and Certain Other Property in Which Iraq Has an Interest."

The so-called "Development Fund for Iraq" was, by the way, one of the most grandiose money-laundering schemes ever devised. All of the profits made from plundering Iraq's oil were to go into this fund, ostensibly for use by the Iraqi people. In fact, this was the clearing-house for payouts to companies like Halliburton and its subsidiary, Kellog Brown & Root.

The 22 May Executive Order reads:

> I, GEORGE W. BUSH, President of the United States of America, find that the threat of attachment or other judicial process against the Development Fund for Iraq, Iraqi petroleum and petroleum products, and interests therein, and proceeds, obligations, or any

financial instruments of any nature whatsoever arising from or related to the sale or marketing thereof, and interests therein, obstructs the orderly reconstruction of Iraq, the restoration and maintenance of peace and security in the country, and the development of political, administrative, and economic institutions in Iraq. This situation constitutes an unusual and extraordinary threat to the national security and foreign policy of the United States and I hereby declare a national emergency to deal with that threat.

I hereby order: Unless licensed or otherwise authorized pursuant to this order, any attachment, judgment, decree, lien, execution, garnishment, or other judicial process is prohibited, and shall be deemed null and void.

This Executive Order, declaring a national emergency, gave complete and total legal cover to Halliburton and every other petroleum and quasi-petroleum corporation currently operating in Iraq. No one can sue them, no one can touch them, no matter what they may do. By Executive Order, George W. Bush released Halliburton and the others from the need to display any kind of responsibility or legal behavior. Halliburton was removed from the sphere of civilization, and the laws that govern civilization, with the stroke of Mr. Bush's pen.

George W. Bush declared a national emergency in this Executive Order for one reason: to lock down the oil, and to give total legal cover to Dick Cheney's Halliburton, so they could do whatever they wanted to get their hands on it, and to get paid for it. Here we have Bush's fingerprints, and here is the reason for not only attacking Wilson, but for chucking up a war that was not necessary.

The Office of Special Plans to the White House Iraq Group, Cheney to Langley, and Bush with his Executive Order; a war to get paid and cash money, honey, for Halliburton and friends. Rove and Libby are small fish. If and when they get fried, the stink may well fill the Oval Office. If George and Dick come out of this unscathed, Mr. Fitzgerald may as well have stayed in Chicago.

RADICAL MILITANT LIBRARIANS
AND OTHER DIRE THREATS

19 DECEMBER 2005

THERE WAS AN INTERNAL FBI email sent in October 2003 that speaks volumes about why our legal system has been arranged the way it has. An unnamed agent was railing via email against the Department of Justice's Office of Intelligence Policy and Review. Specifically, the agent was frustrated by OIPR's failure to deliver authorization to use Section 215 of the Patriot Act for a search. "While radical militant librarians kick us around, true terrorists benefit from OIPR's failure to let us use the tools given to us," wrote the agent.

Radical militant librarians?

Radical militant librarians?

This, right here, is why the legal system is arranged the way it is. This is why officers must obtain warrants from a judge before they can conduct a search. Even in this time of watered-down civil liberties, warrants serve a vital purpose. At a minimum, the warrant firewall keeps walleyed FBI agents with wild hairs about radical militant librarians from bulldozing through the Fourth Amendment.

The President of the United States of America, it seems, does not agree with the sentiment.

It has been widely reported that Bush personally authorized the super-secretive National Security Agency to conduct surveillance against American citizens. "The previously undisclosed decision to permit some eavesdropping inside the country without court approval," wrote the *New York Times* upon breaking the story, "was a major shift in American intelligence-gathering practices, particularly for the National Security Agency, whose mission is to spy on communications abroad. As a result, some officials familiar with the continuing operation have questioned whether the surveillance has stretched, if not crossed, constitutional limits on legal searches."

As if this were not outrageous enough, Bush, during his weekly radio address, bluntly admitted to violating the laws governing surveillance of American citizens and the Fourth Amendment to the Constitution not once, but some 30 times. "I have reauthorized this program more than thirty times since the September 11 attacks," said Bush, "and I intend to do so for as long as our nation faces a continuing threat from al Qaeda and related groups."

These revelations hit Congress like a dung bomb, and caused what would likely have been an easy rubber-stamping of the renewal of the Patriot Act to go flying off the tracks and into the puckerbrush. "Disclosure of the NSA plan had an immediate effect on Capitol Hill," reported the *Washington Post* on Saturday, "where Democratic senators and a handful of Republicans derailed a bill that would renew expiring portions of the USA Patriot Act antiterrorism law. Opponents repeatedly cited the previously unknown NSA program as an example of the kinds of government abuses that concerned them, while the GOP chairman of the Senate Judiciary Committee said he would hold oversight hearings on the issue."

The most disturbing aspect of this situation is, simply, how totally unnecessary it was. The provisions of the Patriot Act, along with several other laws, allow the administration to get warrants for the surveillance of anyone, anywhere in the country, with little trouble. The Foreign Intelligence Surveillance Act (FISA) set up a special court for the dispensation of warrants with no need for evidence or probable cause. This court has almost never denied the issuance of such warrants when asked, and said warrants are usually delivered in a matter of hours.

"Why would the President deliberately circumvent a court that was already wholly inclined to grant him domestic surveillance warrants?" asked columnist David Sirota in a recent essay. "The answer is obvious, though as yet largely unstated in the mainstream media: because the President was likely ordering surveillance operations that were so outrageous, so unrelated to the War on Terror, and, to put it in Constitutional terms, so 'unreasonable' that even a FISA court would not have granted them. This is no conspiracy theory — all the signs point right to this conclusion. In fact, it would be a conspiracy theory to say otherwise, because it would be ignoring the cold, hard facts that we already know."

Retired Air Force Lieutenant Colonel Karen Kwiatkowski, widely known for her revelations about the inner workings of the Pentagon's Office of Special Plans and its manipulation of Iraq war evidence, spent two years working at the National Security Agency. On Sunday, I asked her what the ramifications are of a President throwing aside the firewalls that have blocked governmental surveillance of citizens for the last 25 years.

"It means we are in deep trouble," said Kwiatkowski, "deeper than most Americans really are willing to think about. The safeguards of mid-1970s were put in place by a mobilized Democratic Congress in response to President Richard Nixon's perceived and actual contempt for rule of law, and the other branches of government. At that time, the idea of a sacred Constitution balancing executive power with the legislative power worked to give the Congress both backbone and direction.

"Today," continued Kwiatkowski, "we have a President and administration that has out-Nixoned Nixon in every negative way, with none of the Nixon administration's redeeming attention to detail in domestic and foreign policy. It may indeed mean that the constitution has flat-lined and civil liberties will be only for those who can buy and own a legislator or a political party. We will all need to learn how to spell 'corporate state,' which for Mussolini was his favorable definition of fascism."

I asked Lt. Colonel Kwiatkowski what it all means in the end. "I believe this use of national technical means (NSA communications interceptions) against American citizens is illegal," replied Kwiatkowski, "and I hope the courts will reverse the President. This illegality and misuse of executive power matches that of both the White House Iraq Group and the Office of Special Plans, where the truth and the law were both manipulated in a myriad of ways in order to satisfy an executive desire for domination and destruction of a Baathist Iraq. In all of these cases, American citizens were objectified as means to an end, rather than [treated as] individuals with Creator-granted unalienable rights, safe from excessive government interference and control.

"It all points to growing DC anti-Constitutionalism," concluded Kwiatkowski, "and what Dr. Robert Higgs calls the growth of the warfare state. A warfare state is wholly incompatible with a Constitutional Republic. In my opinion, we need to fight, resist, refuse to subsidize Washington in every way, and we must immediately begin impeachment proceedings against this particular President, not only because he has clearly earned impeachment, but in order to revive a national awareness of the intent of the Founding Fathers to circumscribe centralized state power, and their vision of a free and peaceful Republic."

Hard words—impeachment, warfare state, fascism—for a hard day in our history. King Solomon, whose words bellow from the Book of Proverbs, speaks a warning which George W. Bush may come to know ere long. "He that troubleth his own house," said the King, "shall inherit the wind."

THE REVOLUTION
WAS NOT TELEVISED

31 OCTOBER 2003

THERE WAS A LARGE anti-war rally in Washington last week. The standard slogans were on display for all to see: Impeach Bush, Bring the Troops Home, No Blood for Oil. On the periphery of the protest stood a few dozen "patriots" holding a counter-demonstration in support of Bush and the Iraq war. Among the signs carried by this crew was a banner that succinctly summed up the madness of the age, and the dangerous nature of the current ruling class.

Across the top of the banner, which was clearly professionally made and not hand-lettered, were the block-letter words "SUPPORT PRESIDENT BUSH." Through the center of the banner were black outlines of a fighter aircraft, a tank, an M-16 rifle, a .45 caliber pistol, an attack helicopter, a surface-to-air missile battery, and a thermonuclear bomb. Underneath these images were two more block-letter words: "TRUST JESUS."

The sentiment apparently finds resonance with Senator Trent Lott, Republican of Mississippi. The Wednesday edition of *The Hill* carried a story about GOP concerns over the manner in which the post-war war is unfolding. The trepidation is understandable; more American troops have been killed in the "Mission Accomplished" phase of the war than in the war itself. Lott responded to the crisis in Iraq by saying, "If we have to, we just mow the whole place down, see what happens."

The Bush administration has tried to frame their war as not being a religion-based crusade against the Islamic world. This has been a hard-sell with Muslims, especially since Bush used the word "crusade" immediately after September 11. Norman Podhoretz, one of the ideological fathers of the cadre of hawks currently running our foreign policy, publicly described our conflict in the Mideast as being a process aimed at bringing about "the internal reformation and modernization of Islam." The religious overtones are difficult to miss.

Perhaps the best example of where we stand today comes in the guise of Lt. General William Boykin, Deputy Undersecretary for Defense, who is charged with finding important enemies like Osama bin Laden. Boykin, when not smoking 'em out of their holes, has been touring the fundamentalist pulpits across America. Describing the hunt for a Somali warlord last January, Boykin said, "I knew that my God was bigger than his. I knew that my God was a real God and his was an idol."

Boykin has held forth on the true meaning of the War on Terror. "Satan wants to destroy this nation," says Boykin, "he wants to destroy us as a nation, and he wants to destroy us as a Christian army." In June of 2002, Boykin held up a photograph of Mogadishu to a church congregation. The photo carried the image of a dark spot in the sky above the city. "Ladies and gentlemen," Boykin said, "this is your enemy. It is the principalities of darkness. It is a demonic presence in that city that God revealed to me as the enemy."

The banner carried by the "patriot" in Washington should have had the black outline of an oil well alongside all those weapons. Trusting Jesus has been a lucrative business for some. The Center for Public Integrity released a report on Thursday that details how $8 billion in contracts to "rebuild" Iraq and Afghanistan have gone exclusively to companies that donated piles of money to Bush's 2000 election campaign. These contracts were awarded without the usual bidding process; few beyond the friends of Bush were given the opportunity to cash in on the war.

Most prominent on the list of companies awarded these contacts is Halliburton, the oil company recently run by Vice President Dick Cheney. Halliburton subsidiary Kellog Brown & Root, has gathered to itself a tidy $2.3 billion contract to repair Iraq's oil industry. The price tag for this project was doubled recently by the Bush administration so Halliburton could get a larger share of the $87 billion allocated for Iraq. The reason for the doubling? Halliburton plans to go beyond repairing old oil wells and develop new wells to tap virgin supplies of oil and gas.

Islam is not the only religion to have a militant, fundamentalist Taliban wing making up part of the whole. In America, the Taliban wing of Christianity has assumed power. The banner at that "patriot" rally captures the essence of these frightening extremists: Supporting Bush is placed on the same level as worshipping Jesus, and shot through the middle is the steel fist of weapons and war. September 11 has been refashioned by the Christian Taliban as a rallying cry for an end-times death match against Islam, a rallying cry that obscures the orgy of profiteering that is taking place behind the scenes.

There has been a religiously fundamentalist revolution in the United States. The extremists have taken control of the White House, Congress, the courts, and the military. You did not see this on NBC, ABC, CBS, CNN, MSNBC, CNBC, or Fox, but it happened all the same.

GOING TOO FAR

THE BOUNCER at my bar is named Bob. A native of the deep South, he speaks with the slow drawl of the region, and he is huge. Not outlandishly huge, not freakishly huge, but definitely one of the larger specimens of human one is likely to meet. He works the door at my joint, as well as at another bar down the street a ways.

Each night Bob works he regales my friends and me with stories of mayhem and bouncer-justice, of the drunken boobs stupid enough to think they can push him around at the other establishment. My bar, one gets the sense, is too peaceful for his tastes; he has never been forced to exercise his talents while working there.

Bob and I have assiduously observed the tenets of that invisible sign which hangs over the door of every drinking establishment in America: "Thou Shalt Not Discuss Religion or Politics in This Place." The two reasons for this are straightforward: I don't particularly relish the idea of discussing work when I am in my cups; also, Bob is an ardent Bush supporter, so the first reason becomes doubly significant. If I want to get frustrated and annoyed, I can just turn on CNN and listen to the Know-Nothings ply their wares.

A funny thing happened the other night, however—something that changed the whole dynamic of our relationship. I was passing by Bob, and he grabbed me by the arm to pull me aside. He knows what I do for a living, and wanted to discuss politics in defiance of the invisible sign. "What do you think of the Patriot Act?" he asked me.

"I think it's a damned troubling thing," I said after a moment. "There are aspects of it that have been on the books for years because of the War on Drugs. There are aspects of it that are brand new to American law. Overall, I think it is tremendously invasive and not in line with how we have done things in this country. As a Republican," I said with a bit of the needle in my voice, "the issues of personal freedom and governmental interference should bother you."

"I ain't no Republican," he said. "I'm an Independent. I think they're all crooks."

"Fair enough," I said, "but you are a Bush supporter."

"Yep," he drawled. "So what parts of the Patriot Act don't you like?"

"Well," I said, "one scary part of it is Section 215, the thing people call the "Sneak-and-Peek" provision. Section 215 says law enforcement can enter your house, search your stuff, bug your phone, bug your computer—and they never have to tell you they were there. The FBI could have 215'd their way into my house and I'd never know it. Hell, they could be there right now. All they need to do it is a warrant signed by a judge somewhere."

"That ain't right," he said after a moment's consideration. "But at least they have to talk to a judge."

"Well," I said, "have you heard about all this stuff with the National Security Agency spying on people here in America?"

"Little bit, yeah," he said.

"You know that the NSA can spy on pretty much anyone, tap their phones, do total surveillance?" I asked, and he nodded. "Well, back in 2002, Bush told the NSA to start spying on Americans. Lots of them. But he did this without going through the FISA court."

"FISA court?" he asked.

"FISA stands for the Foreign Intelligence Surveillance Act, which was passed in 1978," I said. "After Watergate and all that craziness, they wanted to make sure our intelligence services weren't being used by people in power to spy on Americans. If you want to get the NSA to spy on Americans, you have to get a warrant from what's called the FISA court. They're a few judges who hear arguments for special FISA warrants."

"OK."

"Now here's one of the crazy parts with this Bush-NSA thing," I said. "To get a warrant from this FISA court, you don't need to have probable cause. You don't need to have evidence. The FISA court has handed out more than 19,000 warrants since it was set up, and has only denied four. And they do it quickly, because obviously if you go before the FISA court for a warrant, you're probably pressed for time. It's the easiest court in America to get a warrant from. Bush totally blew past them, said he didn't need warrants from the FISA court, and just had the NSA start spying away on Americans."

Bob's response to this was too profane to be printed here.

"Why the hell'd he do that?" he finally asked.

"Good question," I said. "There are two probable reasons, neither of which are very comfortable. The first reason is that he and Cheney want to expand the power of the Executive Branch. Cheney, specifically, has always felt that the Executive let go of too much power after Watergate and Vietnam, gave too much power to Congress and the press, and these guys have been trying to get it back. So they decided that since we are 'at war,' they were going to do whatever they damned well pleased."

"Seems smart," he said.

"Maybe," I said, "but that's a different debate. Ask yourself this, though. Imagine a Democrat wins the White House in 2008. These Bush guys will have left this Democrat with outrageously broad powers. His people can spy on whom they like, because Bush did it. They don't have to get warrants, because Bush did it. They can lie to the press, because Bush did it. They can bulldoze Congress, because Bush did it. That make you comfortable?"

"Hell no," he said.

"Right," I said. "Too much power is too much power, no matter who is in power. The separation of powers is there for a reason."

"So what's the other reason you think he didn't get the FISA warrants?" he asked.

"That," I said, "is actually the scarier part. Like I said, FISA has given out those 19,000 warrants and has only denied four. It's incredibly easy to get a warrant from them. Christ, they don't even have to have one of these FISA warrants in hand when they start the surveillance. They can go get one after they're finished. That's part of the FISA law, too. The reason the warrant requirements are there at all is to make sure some crazy maniac in the White House doesn't start spying on Americans, on personal enemies, on you and me. The NSA can do that, so the FISA court is there as a firewall. It's a weak firewall, but it's there."

"OK," he said.

"So maybe," I said, "Bush didn't go to the FISA court because he knew they wouldn't give him the warrants. Maybe he didn't go to the FISA court because he wanted to spy on enemies like Patrick Fitzgerald, like Joe Wilson, like Cindy Sheehan, like Tom Daschle or Harry Reid, or anyone else who was messing with him. Maybe he didn't go to the FISA court because he knew the surveillance he wanted was illegal, but he was damned well going to do it anyway. If this is true, he couldn't go to FISA afterwards and get the warrant."

"That ain't right," said Bob, his face reddening.

"Now take this all one step further," I said, "since you asked about the Patriot Act. Think about that Section 215 and the sneak-and-peek stuff. I told you they need to see a judge first to come into your home, to search and bug your stuff. But this whole NSA deal shows that Bush and these guys don't give a hoot in hell for judges, warrants or the process of law. They're going to do what they want to do, warrant or not. We've got a situation now where Bush and his people could not only be ordering the surveillance of Americans, but could also be authorizing home invasions, and all without any kind of warrants and oversight. What does that sound like to you?"

"Fascism," he said without hesitating.

"This is the reason," I said with a smile, "why I don't talk politics at the bar. I have a way of going on and on until the paint peels. But let me ask you one last question."

"Shoot," he said.

"As a Bush supporter," I said, "how far are you willing to go to support the guy? How much individual liberty, how many laws, are you willing to give up to Bush before we lose the country? How far is too far?"

Bob didn't have anything to say at first. "This," he finally muttered, "is too damned far."

At that moment, a crowd of people came into the bar, and Bob had to check their IDs. I went back to my beer.

Drip, drip, drip.

THE WACK-PACK

13 FEBRUARY 2006

THE BAR I spend my time in enjoys the patronage of quite a cast of characters. My friends and I refer to this crew as the Wack-Pack. On any given night you might see The Eater, Moleman, Shiny, The Living Ham, Earth Pig, The Crotch-Grabber, and the Dick-Washer, among others, bellied up before a beer. There is always a buzz when one of the Pack walks in; it's a fair bet that, soon enough, something strange will transpire.

As odd as these folks are, they are straight-up sane and normal compared to the goofballs, idiots, freaks, and out-and-out maniacs who are staffing the current administration in Washington. I'll take Earth Pig any day over Dick Cheney, who actually blasted a hunting partner in the face with a shotgun down in Texas this weekend. For the record, the last Vice President to shoot someone was Aaron Burr, who put Alexander Hamilton in the ground with a pistol shot in 1804.

This gives a whole new meaning to the idea that the Bush administration is quite literally The Gang That Couldn't Shoot Straight. James Brady, who took a bullet to the back of the head during the attempted assassination of Ronald Reagan, and who went on to found the Brady Campaign to Prevent Gun Violence, released a statement regarding Cheney's prowess with a shotgun on Sunday: "Now I understand why Dick Cheney keeps asking me to go hunting with him. I had a friend once who accidentally shot pellets into his dog—and I thought he was an idiot." His wife, Sarah Brady, piled on by saying, "I've thought Cheney was scary for a long time. Now I know I was right to be nervous."

I guess the NRA is going to have to change its rap. Guns don't kill people. Vice Presidents do. Though, to be fair, the fellow who was shot survived the incident. Harry Whittington, who took the buckshot, should be thankful that Mr. Cheney is in such profoundly ill health. Apparently, Dick Cheney goes hunting these days with a full complement of medical professionals. "After the accident," reported the *New York Times,* "Mr. Cheney's medical attendants helped Mr. Whittington, treating his wounds and covering him in blankets so he would not go into shock." Now that's huntin'.

Another famous member of the Washington Wack-Pack is Attorney General Alberto Gonzales. Gonzales, testifying before the Senate Judiciary Committee regarding warrantless wiretapping of American citizens authorized by Mr. Bush, said, "President Washington, President Lincoln, President Wilson, President Roosevelt have all authorized electronic surveillance on a far broader scale."

Really. George Washington authorized electronic surveillance on a far broader scale than what the National Security Agency is capable of today. How did he do this in an age when the whale-oil lamp was the height of technology? Did he use the old two-cans-and-some-string wiretap trick? Perhaps he was able to bug the Hessians using Ben Franklin's kite and key. The Living Ham and Moleman have said some pretty bizarre things at my bar, but Alberto blew them both out of the water with this one.

George Washington, of course, justified the magical electronic surveillance of Americans by leaning on the broad powers of the unitary executive . . . except he wasn't President yet . . . and there were no Americans yet . . . and, oh yeah, the electron wasn't discovered until 1897. Whatever to all that. If the President does it, it can't be illegal . . . or impossible, for that matter.

Perhaps the wackiest of the Washington Wack-Pack is Defense Secretary Don Rumsfeld, who actually had the gall last week to suggest that weapons of mass destruction were going to be found in Iraq. He said this in front of the National Press Club, no less. "I don't know what we'll find in the months and years ahead," said Rumsfeld. "It could be anything."

Right. It could be anything, except peace or an exit strategy or democracy or freedom. The 26,000 liters of anthrax, the 38,000 liters of botulinum toxin, the 500 tons which is 1 million pounds of sarin, mustard, and VX nerve agent, the 30,000 munitions to deliver the stuff, the mobile biological weapons labs, the al Qaeda connections to 9/11 and the uranium from Niger for use in Iraq's robust nuclear weapons program that Mr. Bush told us about in his January 2003 State of the Union address are definitely still out there . . . but somehow tens of thousands of American soldiers over there, the intelligence professionals over there, the contractors, and the Iraqi police have not managed to find any of it in the 1,061 days since the invasion was first undertaken. Only The Eater could equal this mouthful from Mr. Rumsfeld.

It's funny, but it isn't funny. This is the Wack-Pack that cherry-picked intelligence data to justify a decision to invade Iraq that had already been made, according to former CIA agent Paul Pillar, who was the national intelligence officer for the Near East and South Asia from 2000 to 2005. Four more American soldiers were killed today by a roadside bomb, bringing the death toll to 2,267. The wounded number in the tens of thousands, and the numbers of Iraqi civilians killed and maimed have become, simply, obscene.

This is the Wack-Pack that basically stood back and allowed the city of New Orleans to be destroyed. Michael Brown, the now-disgraced former head of FEMA, testified last week that he alerted senior White House officials, including Chief of Staff Andy Card, that the levees had broken on the Monday it happened. The Bush White House, however, claims they didn't hear about it until the next day. Mr. Bush was too busy strumming a guitar and making ersatz campaign appearances to be bothered with something as piddling as the loss of a major American city.

This is the Wack-Pack that authorized the exposure of a deep-cover CIA agent in order to cover their backsides and eliminate a critic of the war. Lewis Libby has testified to a grand jury that he was authorized by his superiors to expose the name of Valerie Plame in June and July of 2003. This was done after her husband, Ambassador Joseph Wilson, shredded the administration's "uranium from Niger" war rationale in the editorial pages of the *New York Times*. Libby served as Vice President Cheney's chief of staff, so when he refers to being authorized to leak Plame's name by his "superiors," you can bet he is talking about none other than Ol' Shotgun Dick himself.

It's funny, but it isn't funny. Not really. Not at all.

THE NEW FASCISM

The dogmas of the quiet past are inadequate to the stormy present.
The occasion is piled high with difficulty, and we must rise with the
occasion. As our case is new, so we must think anew, and act anew.
We must disenthrall ourselves, and then we shall save our country.

Abraham Lincoln

SAY "FASCISM" to anyone you meet, and you will conjure images of coal-scuttle helmets, of Nazi boot-heels clicking in terrible unison down Berlin streets during dark days that only a few among the living remember. Each day, members of the generation that heard those heels for themselves go into the ground, taking with them whispered words of warning. I saw it for myself, they whisper before they pass. See this tattooed number? See this scar? It happened. It was real.

Say "fascism" to anyone you meet, and you will be greeted with the boilerplate response of the blithely overconfident: Such a thing cannot happen here. This is the United States of America, land of the free and home of the brave. Ours is a nation of laws, of checks and balances, of righteousness and decency. Our laws and traditions stand as a bulwark against the rise of totalitarian madness. It cannot happen here. Thus we are indoctrinated into the school of our own assumed greatness.

"We must disenthrall ourselves," said Abraham Lincoln, and so we must, because it can happen here. It is already happening. All the parroted recitations of grade school civics cannot erase the fact that

77

a new order is rising. Call it "secret fascism" or "smiley-faced fascism." Call it a quiet dictatorship. Call it what you like, but it is here with us in America today, and it is growing.

To be sure, there are no coal-scuttle helmets lined in ranks down our broad avenues, no Tonton Macoute savaging dissidents, no Khmer Rouge slaughtering intellectuals and herding citizens from cities to die by the millions on roads littered with skulls. The core strength of our new fascism is that it speaks softly. It does not present itself in such an obvious way that those who subsist on the dogmas of our greatness can point and say there, there it is, I see it.

This new fascism is not fed only by lies, though to be sure the lies are there in preposterous abundance. This new fascism is fed by myths, our myths, the myths by which we rock ourselves to sleep. This new fascism is in truth an elemental fascism, reborn today by a confluence of events; the diligent work of the few, in combination with the passivity of the many, have brought forth this new order.

The writer Umberto Eco, in a 1995 essay titled "Eternal Fascism: Fourteen Ways of Looking at a Brownshirt," delineated several core elements that have existed in one form or another in every fascist state in history: Parliamentary democracy is by definition rotten, because it does not represent the voice of the people, which is that of the sublime leader. Doctrine outstrips reason, and science is always suspect. The national identity is provided by the nation's enemies. Argument is tantamount to treason. Perpetually at war, the state must govern with the instruments of fear. Citizens do not act; they play the supporting role of "the people" in the grand opera that is the state.

Take these one at a time.

"Parliamentary democracy is by definition rotten, because it does not represent the voice of the people, which is that of the sublime leader."

George W. Bush has all but gelded Congress in recent months, attaching so-called "signing statements" to a variety of laws, which state that the President may act beyond the laws whenever he so chooses. The United States, fashioned as a republic, has as its voice the congressional body. This is all but finished. To cement his victory over the parliamentary system, Bush has put forth one Samuel Alito for the Supreme Court, a man who believes in the ultimate power of the one leader over the many. The balancing branches of government are being refashioned into a satellite system of the executive.

"Doctrine outstrips reason, and science is always suspect."

The supremacy of religious fundamentalism within and without government carries this banner before all others. What is reason in the face of the zealot's faith? Science has become a watered-down vessel for Intelligent Design, and the incontrovertible truths of empirical data are slapped aside.

"The national identity is provided by the nation's enemies."

This has been with us for generations now. Our nation defined ourselves through a comparison to the Nazis, to the Imperial Japanese, and then through decades of comparison to Communism. Terrorism has supplanted all of these, hammered into place on a Tuesday in September by the actions of madmen. We are not them, all is justified in the struggle against them, and so we are defined.

"Argument is tantamount to treason."

All one need do to see this in action is spend some hours with the Fox News channel. Freedom fries. Why do you hate America? You are with us or you are with the terrorists. Watch what you say. Dissent is treasonous.

"Perpetually at war, the state must govern with the instruments of fear."

The manipulation of this population by fear has been ham-fisted, to be sure, but has also been cruelly effective. We do not want the evidence to be a mushroom cloud. Weapons of mass destruction and al Qaeda in Iraq. Nuclear designs in Iran. Plastic sheeting and duct tape. Orange alert. Argument becomes tantamount to treason simply because everyone has been made to feel fear at all times. A frightened populace is easily governed, and governs itself; this lesson was well-learned in the duck-and-cover days of the Cold War. Those lessons have been masterfully applied once again. Today, the citizenry polices itself, and the herd moves as one body. Even the surveillance of innocent citizens by the state is brushed off as a necessary evil. Remember: You are being watched.

"Citizens do not act; they play the supporting role of 'the people' in the grand opera that is the state."

Once, we lived by the vote. Casting a ballot was the single most patriotic duty a citizen could perform, an affirmation of all we held dear and true. Today, we live in the nation of the vanishing voter. Power has been so far removed from the people by those with money and influence that most see voting as a waste of time. Add to this the growing control of the implements of voting and vote-counting by partisan corporations, and the rule of We the People is left in ashes.

We must disenthrall ourselves from the idea that our institutions, our traditions, the barriers that protect us from absolute and authoritarian powers, cannot be broken down. They are being dismantled a brick at a time. The separation of powers has already been annihilated. It is a whispered fascism, not yet marching down your street or pounding upon your door in the dead of night. But it is here, and it is laying deep roots. We must listen beyond the whispered fascism of today to the shouted fascism of tomorrow. We must look beyond the lies and the myths, beyond the dogmas by which we sleep.

HEY, HEY, WOODY GUTHRIE, I WROTE YOU A SONG

28 SEPTEMBER 2005

I'm out here a thousand miles from my home,
Walkin' a road other men have gone down.
I'm seein' your world of people and things,
Your paupers and peasants and princes and kings.
Hey, hey, Woody Guthrie, I wrote you a song
'Bout a funny old world that's a-comin' along.
Seems sick and it's hungry, it's tired and it's torn,
It looks like it's a-dyin' an' it's hardly been born.

Bob Dylan, "Song for Woody"

THE UNBELIEVABLY arrogant and power-mad GOP Representative from Texas, Tom DeLay, got a taste of the whip hand on Wednesday. Indicted on a charge of conspiracy in a campaign finance scheme, DeLay has been forced to step down as Majority Leader in the House. There is no telling how long it will take for the case to wend its way through the courts, but informed opinion puts the time frame at about a year or so. If Tom gets convicted, however, we will never again see his political face. One hopes he saved his bug exterminator equipment. Perhaps, in his new career, he can disprove that old chestnut about not being able to go home again.

Republican Senate Majority Leader Bill Frist is staring down the barrel of an SEC charge that he dumped stock based on insider information. The stock he owned was from HCA, Inc., a company his family founded. Almost immediately after Frist dumped his stock, the value of those holdings dropped 9%. "If there is really any evidence of insider trading, then he's in very serious trouble, and so is his party," said Gary Jacobson, professor of political science at the University of California in San Diego. "It adds another brick to Democrats' argument that Republicans are corrupt." Is it possible that Frist could have been given insider information on a company his own family started? Do the math, and then subtract from Frist's chances of being President in 2008.

A little more than a week ago, the White House's top federal procurement officer, David Safavian, was arrested—not accused, not indicted, but actually slapped with the bracelets—for lying and obstructing a criminal probe against super-lobbyist Jack Abramoff. Safavian is part of a larger investigation surrounding Abramoff's indictment on charges of wire fraud and conspiracy. The names flying around these charges include GOP Rep. Robert Ney of Ohio, former Christian Coalition leader Ralph Reed, and anti-tax crusader Grover Norquist. Had Safavian not resigned his White House post on the day he was arrested, they would have clapped him in irons right there inside 1600 Pennsylvania. Sic semper moral majority.

Oh yeah, and there's still that pesky matter of the investigation into an outed CIA agent floating around. According to a variety of reputable and rock-solid sources, folks in the White House are decidedly unhappy and nervous about this one. What on earth is the world coming to? These guys control the government, right? They control all the agencies responsible for these kinds of investigations. Despite that, DeLay and Frist and Safavian and Abramoff and Lord only knows who else are getting a crash course in the justice system.

And how is Mr. Bush coping through all this? One answer can be found in this week's *Newsweek,* which describes George watching Hurricane Rita like a hawk after the Katrina debacle. "His eyes," reads the *Newsweek* piece, "were puffy from lack of sleep (he had been awakened all through the night with bulletins), and he seemed cranky and fidgety. A group of reporters and photographers had been summoned by White House handlers to capture a photo op of the commander in chief at his post. Bush stared at them balefully. He rocked back and forth in his chair, furiously at times, asked no questions and took no notes. It almost seemed as though he resented having to strike a pose for the press."

Rocked back and forth? Furiously at times? Sounds like a pathological response. I guess 40% approval ratings across the board will do that. These guys are sharp, though. They'll dig their way out. Or will they? On Monday, just before the DeLay indictment came out, the White House released a statement of support. "Majority Leader DeLay is someone the president considers a friend," read the statement. "The president looks forward to continuing to work closely with the majority leader to get things done on behalf of the American people."

Oops. Keep rocking, George.

The *Washington Post*'s Terry Neal published an article titled "Echoes of 1994 with Current Scandals?" on Tuesday. "Is it 1994 all over again?" asked Neal. "Dark and ominous clouds are gathering over the Republican Party these days, with a series of ethical and legal scandals that threaten to further damage a White House and Congress already reeling from a sharp drop in public approval ratings. On top of all of that, a special prosecutor and grand jury continue to investigate what, if any, role White House officials may have played in the leaking of the name of a covert operative to reporters. And the White House has come under increasing scrutiny, in the wake of the Hurricane Katrina fiasco, for rampant cronyism in its appointments to top level jobs, including director of the Federal Emergency Management Agency and nominees for head of Immigration and Customs Enforcement and deputy attorney general, among others."

Somewhere close to a half million people showed up in Washington last weekend to shout the White House down. A variety of organizations, such as Progressive Democrats of America, held conventions to plan their electoral strategies for 2006. On Monday, hundreds of activists swarmed House offices on Capitol Hill to demand an exit from Iraq. The anti-war movement, dismissed as non-existent by the GOP, has gained strength and speed with the actions of heroes like Cindy Sheehan, who got herself arrested on Monday for praying in front of the White House.

Woody Guthrie used to paint "This Machine Kills Fascists" on his guitars. I think he'd be pleased to see how fast the rock has started rolling down the hill.

THE SUPREMACY
OF THE SUPER-CITIZEN

30 JUNE 2005

Unless you become more watchful in your States and check this
spirit of monopoly and thirst for exclusive privileges, you will in the
end find that the most important powers of Government have been
given or bartered away, and the control of your dearest interests
have been passed into the hands of these corporations.

Andrew Jackson, farewell address, 04 March 1837

THE DOCUMENT READS, "All men are created equal." When those words were first put to paper, of course, the literal meaning of the phrase did not match what was written. A more accurate sentence would have read, "All white, land-owning men are created equal," but despite the inherent racism and misogyny buried in the original meaning, the words had magic and power enough to lay the groundwork for 200 years of progress.

The words as written became the basis for reform after reform, for the strengthening of the rights of minorities, women, and basically anyone who would be made subservient to anyone else. The struggle took a long time, and continues today with much remaining to do before that equality is truly achieved, but the strength of those words as written has been proven time and again to be more than a match for anyone who would stand on the neck of a fellow citizen.

That's what the billboard reads, anyway. That's the propaganda, the myth, the way we rock ourselves to sleep at night. The truth is significantly different, however, and is at the root of just about every-thing that has gone wrong with this great democratic experiment.

We are not all created equal, in fact. This inequality is not based on race, or sex, or religion, but upon the slow development of a body of laws that have created and empowered a breed of super-citizens who rule over every aspect of our lives, almost completely beyond the reach of justice. These super-citizens exist today under the familiar name "corporation."

But wait, a corporation is basically a company, right? A corpora-tion is a non-living entity, a group of people endeavoring to make money in a business enterprise or non-profit organization, right? Wrong. A corporation is indeed a non-living entity, a group of people looking to make money. But thanks to a Supreme Court decision, corporations are also actual living entities in every legal sense of the word, with all rights and privileges of citizenship—and several more besides—intact.

A SHORT HISTORY OF CORPORATIONS

The word "corporation" comes from the Latin "corpus," or "body." The *Oxford English Dictionary* defines "corporation" as, "A group of people authorized to act as an individual." The history of corpora-tions in America is intertwined with the story of the revolution that birthed this nation. British corporations in colonial America were rebelled against vigorously as representatives of the Crown, which they were.

Many of the principal actors in the American Revolution, among them George Washington, wanted to throw off British rule because they felt their ability to conduct commerce freely was being dis-rupted. When 60 Boston residents hurled the tea into Boston Harbor in 1773, it was an attack specifically upon the economic power and supremacy of a corporation called the British East India Tea Company, which had been undercutting the profits of colonial mer-chants thanks to the passage of the Tea Acts.

After the revolution, and for a hundred years, the American people bore a deep distrust of the corporation, and corporations were regulated severely. Corporate charters were created by individual states, and those states had the power to revoke that charter if the corporation was deemed to be acting against the public good or had deviated from its charter. Corporations were not allowed to own other corporations, nor were they allowed to participate in the political process.

Very slowly over that 100 years, however, the power of the corporation began to grow. In the 1818 Supreme Court case *Dartmouth College v. Woodward*, Daniel Webster, advocating for Dartmouth, argued passionately for the power of corporations in regards to property rights. The Court sided with Webster and corporate rights, stating, "The opinion of the Court, after mature deliberation, is that this corporate charter is a contract, the obligation of which cannot be impaired without violating the Constitution of the United States. This opinion appears to us to be equally supported by reason, and by the former decisions of this Court."

A good deal of hell was raised after this decision, with many citizens and state legislatures standing upon the right of a state to repeal or amend a corporate charter. Seven years later, however, another Supreme Court case buttressed the power of the corporation with their decision in *Society for the Preservation of the Gospel in Foreign Parts v. Town of Pawlet*. The Society was seeking to protect its colonial-era property grants in Vermont, while Vermont was seeking to revoke those grants. The Court decided in favor of the Society, and explicitly extended the same protections to corporation-owned property as are enjoyed by property-owning natural persons.

Corporations in America began to become truly powerful with the rise of the railroads. Railroads were the lifeblood of the growing nation, carrying both agriculture and industry from one side of the country to the other. This was a highly profitable enterprise, and railroad corporations began to exert heavy influence on both state and federal leaders. Corporate attorneys boldly asserted the precedents set in the Dartmouth and Society Supreme Court decisions, demanding that corporations deserved to have at least some of the rights of natural persons. Meanwhile, attorneys loyal to the railroads began to rise through the ranks of the judiciary, finally finding seats on the highest bench.

This process came to a final head in 1886, when the Supreme Court heard the case *Santa Clara County v. Southern Pacific Railroad*. Arguments over the rights of corporations as persons had been raging for decades, and Chief Justice Waite pounded home the nail: "The court does not wish to hear argument on the question whether the provision in the Fourteenth Amendment to the Constitution, which forbids a State to deny to any person within its jurisdiction the equal protection of the laws, applies to these corporations. We are all of the opinion that it does."

"WE ARE OF THE OPINION THAT IT DOES"

The pertinent section of the Fourteenth Amendment reads, "All persons born or naturalized in the United States, and subject to the jurisdiction thereof, are citizens of the United States and of the State wherein they reside. No State shall make or enforce any law which shall abridge the privileges or immunities of citizens of the United States; nor shall any State deprive any person of life, liberty, or property, without due process of law; nor deny to any person within its jurisdiction the equal protection of the laws."

Before the Santa Clara decision, this amendment applied only to living, breathing people. After Santa Clara, it applied also to massively wealthy corporations, groups of people authorized to act as individuals, but beyond the kinds of legal liabilities natural persons are subject to. The Santa Clara decision, and subsequent decisions affirming it, created the formidable distinction between the citizen and the super-citizen.

Both have purchasing power, both can give money to whomever or whatever they please, but the difference lies in the extent to which this can be done. A natural person can buy a house and give money to a politician. A wealthy corporation, on the other hand, can buy a thousand houses and give money to a thousand politicians. In other words, a corporation that enjoys the same rights as a natural person has a thousand times the power and influence of a natural person over the economics and politics of the country. That is a super-citizen.

Because these super-citizens can exert so much power, their rights have been dramatically extended over the years. In the 1950s, for example, corporations paid some 40% of the taxes in this country. They flexed their muscles and exerted their influence, and by 1980 were paying only 26% of the taxes in this country. The Economic Recovery Tax Act of 1981 slashed that payment to 8%.

The economic boon enjoyed by these super-citizens is augmented by the fact that regular citizens' tax dollars are used by the government to purchase goods and services from corporations involved in the production of weapons, petroleum, timber, and agricultural products. Corporate perks like jets, elaborate headquarters, public relations firms, and executive retreats are all tax write-offs; the regular citizen, by contrast, pays for their perks with after-tax dollars. When a corporation screws up and destroys an ecosystem with a toxic spill, corporate liability shields protect them from financial and legal punishment, and the cost of the clean-up is borne by the tax dollars of the regular citizen.

Today, corporations control almost every aspect of what we see, hear, eat, wear, and live. Every television news media organization is owned by a small handful of corporations, which use these news outlets to filter out information that might be damaging to the parent company. Agriculture in America is controlled by a small group of corporations. One cannot drive a car, rent a van, buy a house or deliver goods in a business transaction without purchasing insurance from a corporation. Getting sick in America has become a ruinously expensive experience because corporations now control even the smallest functions of the medical profession, and have turned the practice of health care into a for-profit industry.

The influence these super-citizens hold over local, state and national politics is the reason why so many privileges have been afforded to them. This influence has existed to one degree or another for decades. Yet it was another Supreme Court decision, handed down in 1976, that allowed these super-citizens to establish a stranglehold on our politics and government institutions.

THE SUPREMACY OF THE SUPER-CITIZEN

In 1976, the case *Buckley v. Valeo* came before the Supreme Court. Senator James Buckley, former Senator and Presidential candidate Eugene McCarthy and several others had filed suit to challenge the constitutionality of the Federal Election Campaign Act of 1971 (FECA) and the Presidential Election Campaign Fund Act. Among the defendants were Francis Valeo—Secretary of the Senate and *ex officio* member of the newly created Federal Election Commission— as well as the Commission itself.

The final Supreme Court decision split a number of legal hairs. The decision upheld the constitutionality of limiting political contributions to candidates, and the disclosure and record-keeping requirements established by FECA. The aspects of FECA deemed unconstitutional, however, became the basis for the supremacy of the super-citizen. In short, the Court decided that limiting the amount of money a candidate could spend was a violation of the First Amendment. In other words, the spending of campaign money was equated with the right of free speech.

On the surface, the decision makes sense. Because so much of modern political campaigning involves television and radio advertisements, direct mailing of campaign literature, extensive travel and lodging, staff payrolls, and (because all these things cost money) a limitation on campaign spending necessarily restricts the ability of a candidate to practice free speech in the political realm.

The danger, of course, was that corporations would take advantage of the new spending freedoms enjoyed by politicians and flood them with influence-creating cash. The Court attempted to address this concern by upholding the limits on contribution amounts, stating that these limitations were the "primary weapons against the reality or appearance of improper influence stemming from the dependence of candidates on large campaign contributions."

The Court's attempt to address this concern failed, in no small part because of the existence of so-called "soft money." Soft money was supposed to be cash given to political parties for "party-building activities," rather than for the direct support of candidates and campaigns. Soft money contributions were not subjected to limitations, allowing super-citizens to flood outrageous amounts of money into the process. Because the soft-money rules were so vague, and because soft money contributions were so huge, the money was invariably directed towards the support of individual candidates. The politicians became corporate entities, commodities bought and sold by the super-citizens.

The passage in 2002 of the Campaign Reform Act did little to cut into the massive influence in politics enjoyed by the super-citizens. The Campaign Reform Act made most soft money contributions illegal, but created a loophole large enough to sail a British tea ship through with the enshrinement of 527 groups as political entities. So-called 527s are tax-exempt organizations created to influence the nomination, election, appointment, or defeat of political candidates.

The soft money previously given to political parties goes now to these groups, and these groups enjoy umbilical connections to the parties and candidates they work in favor of. In other words, nothing really changed and the influence of the super-citizens was undiminished. The Campaign Reform Act also raised the hard money contribution limit from $1,000 to $2,000, thus doubling the ability of super-citizens to exert direct financial influence upon candidates and office-holders.

Today, virtually every politician holding national office is financially beholden to a corporation. Beyond the favorable tax status for corporations established by these owned politicians, the effects of this ownership are felt by average citizens every day.

Foreign policy is all too often decided by corporate considerations, and these decisions often lead to war. The air we breathe, the food we eat, and the water we drink is contaminated by pollutants that corporations are legally allowed to spew, thanks to the legislative protections created by corporate-owned politicians. Draconian sentencing rules created by legislators that incarcerate millions of Americans—think "The War on Drugs" specifically—have as much to do with the influence of the corporate-controlled prison industry as with anything else.

This list goes on and on. Super-citizens define our reality by controlling the information we receive via television, newspaper, and radio. Super-citizens make sure that information casts them in a favorable light. Super-citizens pound us with advertising and thus maintain the fiction that spending money on products defines the nature of a person.

The best and brightest are drafted out of law school to work for corporate defense firms for six-figure salaries, thus ensuring that super-citizens enjoy a level of legal defense not available to anyone else. Many of these corporate attorneys graduate to the bench, where they extend the influence of super-citizens across all levels of the judicial branch.

More than anything else, however, super-citizens control the ways and means of government at every level. They bought it, they own it, and they make sure it does their bidding. The needs, requirements, and best interests of the average citizen do not enter into the equation.

CREATED EQUAL

Arguments can be made that corporations are good for the economy and the country. They can get things done with a speed and efficiency not often found in the bureaucracies of government. When the country had to get itself ready to fight World War II, for one example, it was the industrial and manufacturing corporations that produced the means to achieve victory beyond anyone's expectations.

In the final analysis, however, the influence held by these entities is antithetical to the fundamental ideals of the nation. We are not all created equal, and within that inequality lies the potential for enormous evil. Consider the case of I.G. Farben, the industrial giant that was the financial core of the Nazi regime. Farben produced the gas used in the concentration camps, and made lucrative use of slave labor in the camps. Before the war, Farben worked hand-in-hand with a number of powerful American corporations, the most prominent of which was Standard Oil.

In the aftermath of World War II, the crimes committed by Farben were considered so enormous that many wanted the corporation to be utterly destroyed. Instead, Farben was split into several smaller entities, several of which still exist. Millions of Americans purchase aspirin from Bayer, a company that was once part of Farben. Commercials for BASF tell us that company makes the products we buy better, but do not tell us that BASF was once part of Farben. It speaks to the power enjoyed by corporations to consider that Farben, which forced concentration camp laborers to manufacture the Zyklon-B used to exterminate them and which was the backbone of Nazi financial power, was not destroyed out of hand once the war was over. Farben is still with us. Its charter has merely been changed.

Are all corporations on the moral level of I.G. Farben? Certainly not. Many corporations work for the public good, and many that work for their own enrichment do not necessarily undermine the country and its principles. But some do, and they exist beyond punishment or account.

The potential for evil is certainly there when super-citizens exist above the law. When the *New York Times* reviewed the book *The Crime and Punishment of I.G. Farben,* it observed that the story of Farben "forces one to consider the possibility that when corporate evil reaches a certain status, it simply cannot be defeated."

In the end, the existence of incredibly powerful entities that enjoy the status of citizens demotes the vast majority of average citizens to second-class status. If the ideals we hold sacred have any truth to them, if the myths we sleep by have any basis in reality, such a division is intolerable and must be changed. "All men are created equal" once excluded vast swaths of Americans from their basic rights. Battles were fought to change that. Today, a battle to realign the balance of power between the citizen and the super-citizen must also be fought. And it must be won.

THE STORY OF THE GHOST

31 JANUARY 2005

United States officials were surprised and heartened today at the
size of turnout in South Vietnam's presidential election despite a
Vietcong terrorist campaign to disrupt the voting. According to
reports from Saigon, 83 percent of the 5.85 million registered voters
cast their ballots yesterday. Many of them risked reprisals threatened
by the Vietcong. A successful election has long been seen as the key-
stone in President Johnson's policy of encouraging the growth of
constitutional processes in South Vietnam.

New York Times article by Peter Grose titled,
"U.S. Encouraged by Vietnam Vote," 04 September 1967

IN ALL THE MEDIA hoopla over Sunday's "election" in Iraq, a few
details got missed.

The powerful and influential Association of Muslim Scholars is
not buying the idea that there was some great democratic break-
through with this vote. AMS spokesman Muhammad al-Kubaysi
responded to the election by saying, "The elections are not a solution
to the Iraqi problem, because this problem is not an internal dispute
to be resolved through accords and elections. It lies in the presence
of a foreign power that occupies this country and refuses even the
mere scheduling of the withdrawal of its forces from Iraq."

"We have consistently argued," continued al-Kubaysi, "that elections can only occur in a democracy that enjoys sovereignty. Our
sovereignty is incomplete. Our sovereignty is usurped by foreign
forces that have occupied our land and hurt our dignity. These

elections . . . are a means of establishing the foreign forces in Iraq and keeping Iraq under the yoke of occupation. They should have been postponed."

Al-Kubaysi likewise raised grave concerns about low turnout in Sunni areas such as Baghdad, Baquba, and Samarra, and stated flatly that the deep secrecy that shrouded the candidates themselves invalidated the process. "The voter goes to the polling stations not knowing who he is voting for in the first place," he said. "There are more than 7,700 candidates, and I challenge any Iraqi voter to name more than half a dozen. Their names have not been announced but have been kept secret. Elections should never have been held under these present circumstances."

The American media is painting these newly-minted Iraqi voters as flush with the thrill of casting a ballot. In truth, however, some other more pressing motivations lay behind their rush to the polling places. Dahr Jamail, writing for Inter Press Service, reported that "Many Iraqis had expressed fears before the election that their monthly food rations would be cut if they did not vote. They said they had to sign voter registration forms in order to pick up their food supplies. Just days before the election, 52-year-old Amin Hajar, who owns an auto garage in central Baghdad, had said, 'I'll vote because I can't afford to have my food ration cut. If that happened, me and my family would starve to death.'"

"Will Vote for Food" is not a spectacular billboard for the export of democracy.

"Where there was a large turnout," continued Jamail, "the motivation behind the voting and the processes both appeared questionable. The Kurds up north were voting for autonomy, if not independence. In the south and elsewhere Shias were competing with Kurds for a bigger say in the 275-member national assembly. In some places like Mosul the turnout was heavier than expected. But many of the voters came from outside, and identity checks on voters appeared lax. Others spoke of vote-buying bids. More than 30 Iraqis, a U.S. soldier, and at least 10 British troops died Sunday.

Hundreds of Iraqis were also wounded in attacks across Baghdad, in Baquba 50km northeast of the capital as well as in the northern cities Mosul and Kirkuk."

Perhaps the most glaring indication that this "election" did little to settle the bloody reality in Iraq came three days before the ballots were cast. In a letter to Congress dated 28 January, the neoconservative think-tank/power broker known as the Project for the New American Century (PNAC) essentially called for a draft without actually using the "d" word.

Project Censored, the organization that tracks important yet wildly under-reported stories, declared the existence, motivations, and influence of PNAC to be the number one censored media story for 2002–2003.

The first vital fact one needs to know about PNAC has to do with its membership roll call: Dick Cheney, Vice President of the United States, former CEO of Halliburton; Donald Rumsfeld, Secretary of Defense; Paul Wolfowitz, Deputy Secretary of Defense; Elliot Abrams, National Security Council; John Bolton, Undersecretary for Arms Control and International Security; I. Lewis Libby, Cheney's top National Security assistant. This list goes on.

These people didn't enjoy those fancy titles in 2000, when the PNAC manifesto "Rebuilding America's Defenses" was first published. Before 2000, these men were just a bunch of power players who got shoved out of government in 1993. In the time that passed between Clinton and those hanging chads, these people got together in PNAC and laid out a blueprint. "Rebuilding America's Defenses" was the ultimate result. The year 2000 became 2001, and the PNAC boys suddenly had the fancy titles and a chance to swing some weight.

"Rebuilding America's Defenses" became the roadmap for foreign policy decisions made in the White House and the Pentagon; PNAC had the Vice President's office in one building, and the Defense Secretary's office in the other. Attacking Iraq was central to that roadmap from the beginning. When former counterterrorism czar Richard Clarke accused the Bush administration of focusing on Iraq to the detriment of addressing legitimate threats, he was essentially denouncing them for using the attacks of September 11 as an excuse to execute the PNAC blueprint.

The goals codified in "'Rebuilding America's Defenses," the manifesto, can be boiled down to a few sentences: The invasion and occupation of Iraq, for reasons that had nothing to do with Saddam Hussein; the building of several permanent military bases in Iraq, the purpose of which is to telegraph force throughout the region; the takeover by Western petroleum corporations of Iraq's nationalized oil industry; and the ultimate destabilization and overthrow of a variety of regimes in the Middle East, friend and foe alike, by military or economic means, or both.

"Indeed," it is written on page 14 of "Rebuilding America's Defenses," "the United States has for decades sought to play a more permanent role in Gulf regional security. While the unresolved conflict with Iraq provides the immediate justification, the need for a substantial American force presence in the Gulf transcends the issue of the regime of Saddam Hussein."

In the last five years, PNAC has achieved every single thing it placed on its wish list back in 2000. This is why their letter to Congress last week is so disturbing. The letter reads in part:

> The United States military is too small for the responsibilities we are asking it to assume. Those responsibilities are real and important. They are not going away. The United States will not and should not become less engaged in the world in the years to come. But our national security, global peace and stability, and the defense and promotion of freedom in the post-9/11 world require a larger military force than we have today. The administration has unfortunately resisted increasing our ground forces to the size needed to meet today's (and tomorrow's) missions and challenges.
>
> So we write to ask you and your colleagues in the legislative branch to take the steps necessary to increase substantially the size of the active duty Army and Marine Corps. While estimates vary about just how large an increase is required, and Congress will make its own determination as to size and structure, it is our judgment that we should aim for an increase in the active duty

Army and Marine Corps, together, of at least 25,000 troops each year over the next several years.

Article 1, Section 8 of the Constitution places the power and the duty to raise and support the military forces of the United States in the hands of the Congress. That is why we, the undersigned, a bipartisan group with diverse policy views, have come together to call upon you to act. You will be serving your country well if you insist on providing the military manpower we need to meet America's obligations, and to help ensure success in carrying out our foreign policy objectives in a dangerous, but also hopeful, world.

Brush aside the patriotic language, and you have the ideological architects of this disastrous Iraq invasion stating flatly that the American military is being bled dry, and that the ranks must be replenished before that military can be used to push into Iran, Syria, and the other targeted nations. The "d" word is not in this letter, but it screams out from between the lines. All the lip service paid to the Iraq elections by these people does not contrast well with their cry for more warm bodies to feed into the meat grinder.

Lyndon Johnson was excited about voter turnout in Vietnam in September 1967. Eight years, three Presidents, and millions of dead people later, that excitement proved to have been wretchedly illusory. There is no reason, no reason whatsoever, to believe that the Iraq election we witnessed this weekend will bring anything other than death and violence to the people of that nation and our soldiers who move among them. History repeats itself only when we are stupid enough to miss the lessons learned in past failures. The wheel is coming around again.

GET SOME

"GET SOME."

That's what Marines say before the shooting starts, before the metal meets the meat, before the difference between Now and Later becomes a matter of survival and strength.

Get some, they say. Get some.

The time has come for the soldiers, those who have completed their service and those who stand the watch today, to get some. Not in a firefight, not in a desert or a jungle or on a frozen plain, not on any battlefield soaked with blood and rent with screams, but on a field of honor where the good name and sacrifice and suffering of our soldiers has become all too easily slapped aside in a quest to salvage poll numbers and approval ratings.

That's the deal, you know. That's what the political pushers mean when they speak of "staying the course" in Iraq.

The political pushers know this invasion and occupation has been a catastrophe. They know the people in Iraq don't want us there. They know the intelligence was cooked. They know about the Office of Special Plans and the White House Iraq Group. They know about Curveball, about Ibn al-Shaykh al-Libi, about fake documents out of Niger falsely prophesying mushroom clouds, about outed CIA agents and blown networks and the end of Brewster Jennings; they know about British intelligence dossiers that were little more than plagiarized magazine articles, and about weapons of mass destruction that had been destroyed years before. They know now, and they knew then.

The political pushers know our armed services are bleeding to death. They know recruitment is at an all-time low. They know experienced Reservists and officers are walking away because the burden is too great for any man or woman to bear. They know what Spc. Jose Navarette from Odessa, Texas, knows as he stands the watch in Tikrit. "This whole war is like a modern-day Vietnam," said Navarette. "You see more people dying every day. That makes you wonder if it's worthwhile."

The political pushers know all this, but push "stay the course" anyway. They don't say this because they believe it, or because they want to honor the fallen in Iraq by "completing the mission." The soldiers have already completed the mission, 2,097 have died for the mission, tens of thousands more have been ripped up for the mission, they all did what they were ordered to do, but it's "stay the course" we hear.

The political pushers know that "completing the mission" has nothing to do with democracy in Iraq or timetables for withdrawal or anything else. They know that "stay the course" means one thing: making sure Bush and his congressional allies don't suffer another political setback before the '06 midterm elections. That's it and that's all, and they know.

Here's what they don't know.

They don't know what blood smells like when it is mixed with mud and sand. They don't know what it sounds like when a bullet strikes flesh, what a blade sounds like when it grinds against bone, what it feels like to be in the dark and far from home with only a rifle and a teammate between them and a hole in the ground and a folded flag.

They don't know what the kick of adrenaline before the shooting starts feels like, what the sound of 100 men bellowing "Get some!" sounds like, what you do with your hands when they start to shake after the noise and thunder and dying is done with, until the next time.

Millions of Americans don't know about that, and never will, but there is one crucial difference. Those millions of Americans don't pretend to know, don't act like they've been there, don't throw soldiers into early graves under the false pretense of hard wisdom they will never earn. The political pushers of this Iraq occupation, those who preach "staying the course" and "completing the mission" pretend to know, and would dare to lecture and scold anyone who would disagree. But they don't know.

John Murtha knows. He joined the Marine Corps in 1952, served in uniform for 37 years, and rose to the rank of colonel. During his service, he volunteered for Vietnam. Before he was done, he was awarded the Bronze Star with Combat "V," two Purple Hearts, and the Vietnamese Cross of Gallantry. Upon his retirement from the Marines in 1990, he was awarded the Navy Distinguished Service Medal by the Commandant of the Marine Corps.

John Murtha knows, and when he stood before the House of Representatives last week as one of that body's longest-serving members to tell the truth about Iraq, he spoke from the well of that knowledge. "It is time for a change in direction," he said, choking back tears. "Our military is suffering. The future of our country is at risk. We cannot continue on the present course. It is evident that continued military action in Iraq is not in the best interests of the United States of America, the Iraqi people or the Persian Gulf region."

How was this decorated hero greeted after his remarks? He was called reprehensible and irresponsible by Dick Cheney, a man who took five deferments to stay away from the war Murtha volunteered to fight. He was called a coward. Only after these slanders were greeted with universal condemnation were they grudgingly retracted. That bell, however, cannot be un-rung. They called John Murtha a coward, these people who do not know what he knows. They called him a coward.

If these political pushers can throw a man like John Murtha under the bus, they can do it to anyone. The sacred honor earned by those who have served this country in the uniform of our military, those who have stood the watch and heard the screams and felt that place inside go empty and cold and strange when they know they have taken the life of another person, the sacred honor of those who know, means nothing to the pushers. Nothing at all. They will rubbish men like John Murtha, they will consign hundreds or thousands of soldiers to death and maiming, they will allow the Armed Services of the United States to become a hollowed-out shell.

They will do all this to protect their poll numbers. That is what "staying the course" means. That's all it has ever meant.

The time has come for the soldiers, those who have completed their service and those who stand the watch today, to get some.

LET THE DEAD
TEACH THE LIVING

08 SEPTEMBER 2005

THEY HAVE TURNED a gigantic warehouse into a makeshift morgue in the Louisiana town of St. Gabriel. Doctors and forensic specialists wait there for the bodies to come in, bodies with no identification, bodies that have spent days submerged in water, bodies gnawed by dogs and rats and 'gators. The doctors have posted a hand-lettered sign on the wall: "Mortui Vivis Praecipant." It means, "Let the dead teach the living."

There's a stiffened body under a tarp on Union Street in downtown New Orleans that has been there for days. Others float helplessly down streets and in canals. More than 100 people died in a warehouse down by the docks. They had been waiting for a rescue that never came. Thirty people died in a flooded-out nursing home outside the city, left there by the staff to wait for a rescue that, again, never came. By every indication, there are thousands of other bodies awaiting discovery, people who lost their lives in exactly this fashion. FEMA has ordered 25,000 body bags.

An edict has come down from the federal government banning press photographers from taking any pictures of the dead as they lie waiting for removal. Echoes of the ban on photographs of American soldiers in flag-draped caskets returned from Iraq are present, as are echoes of a ban on the new photos taken from within Abu Ghraib.

Perhaps it is thought that if the American people cannot see death, they will come to believe it does not exist.

Four people have died already from water-borne disease. *Vibrio vulnificus,* a bacterium naturally found in salt water, killed one person plucked from the city who was then taken to Texas, and killed three people removed to Mississippi. The bacterium is a close cousin to cholera. Tests on the standing water in New Orleans have found more than 100 different chemicals present, including pesticides and solvents. Lead is also present in dangerous levels. The waters contain at least ten times the amount of acceptable bacterial strains found in sewage. The phrase "at least ten times" must be used, because the tests themselves are unable to register anything higher than that. The bacteria, in other words, pegged the needle.

A first-hand account from a professional psychologist named Shari Julian is making the rounds. Julian traveled to New Orleans to volunteer her time in rescue and rehabilitation efforts in Reunion Arena and the Civic Center. "I am no infection guru," reported Julian, "but as soon as I heard on day one that people with no water were forced to drink water with bloated bodies, feces, and rats in it, the thought of cholera, typhoid, and delayed disease immediately occurred to me. What if the fears of disease are correct? People are fanning out throughout America. Where is the CDC?

"The trauma they are experiencing," continued Julian, "is so profound that we have no cultural term or machinery set up for it. The dead and nameless bodies by the thousands rotting in the water, arriving dead on the buses with them, or dying next to them in the shelters, are a huge festering wound that no one dares mention. This is a true Diaspora the likes of which we haven't seen since Reconstruction. The immediate needs that are being addressed ignore the greater traumas yet to be spoken. No governmental system can survive the number of wounded and disillusioned people that we are going to see sprouting up all over America. Something far greater and more organized has to be done."

Professor, author, and columnist Walter Brasch has compiled

some numbers that deserve to be included in any discussion of what
has taken place. George W. Bush inherited from his predecessor a
$230 billion budget surplus and a balanced budget. In the five years
since, the surplus has become a $7.9 trillion deficit, which increases
at a rate of about $1.7 billion per day. The occupation of Iraq costs
somewhere between $4 billion and $5 billion per month, increasing
the deficit exponentially. A meticulously reconstructed Federal
Emergency Management Agency was downsized and budget-
slashed by this administration as part of its "small-government"
quest, and run by an appointee whose experience in disaster management came from representing the owners of Arabian horses.

Mortui Vivis Praecipant. What have the dead taught the living in
the last two weeks? We have learned that priorities matter. We have
learned that the conservative small-government model is a recipe for
catastrophe. We have learned that government is sure to absolutely
fail its citizens when it is run by people who hate government. We
have learned that massive budget cuts and agency downsizing are
not theoretical or political exercises. Before Katrina, we were learning that an irresponsible and unnecessary war in Iraq was making us
less safe at home. After Katrina, we have learned exactly how unsafe
we are as four years of tough talk about defending the nation has
been exposed by the wind and the rain. We have learned that leadership matters, and that the absence of leadership is deadly.

We have been hearing from Bush and his friends that now is not a
time for the "Blame Game," as if an assessment of responsibility is
nothing more than another political football to be punted down the
field. A *New York Times* editorial from Wednesday stated, "This is not
a game. It is critical to know what 'things went wrong,' as Mr. Bush
put it. But we also need to know which officials failed—not to
humiliate them, but to replace them with competent people . . .
Disasters like this are not a city or a state issue. They concern the
entire nation and demand a national response—certainly a better
one than the White House comments that 'tremendous progress'
had been made in Louisiana."

Never fear, however, for George W. Bush has said he will personally investigate the failures that led to this calamity. This is a comforting thought. Perhaps he will appoint Henry Kissinger, whom Bush first chose to head the investigation into 9/11 way back when, to lead the way.

This has only just begun. The impact of hundreds of thousands of displaced people, who need jobs and homes and whose children need schooling, will slowly but surely begin to be felt. The psychological scars from the experience will begin to tell upon them. "We are more vulnerable now than before 9/11 because faith in the system is gone" reported Shari Julian from New Orleans. "No system can sustain itself as a viable entity when the citizenry are the walking wounded. Victims implode a system from within and expose its decay. This is the beginning of the end unless we can get a drastic change of philosophy and restore the government to a system "by the people for the people." Right now nobody down here believes we have that."

What have the dead taught the living? Responsible and effective government matters. At this moment, we have neither. We are, simply put, on our own.

BUSH'S SOVIET STATE

22 JULY 2005

IT'S FUNNY in an awful sort of way. The defining events of the last 50 years all centered around the Cold War and the eventual demise of the Soviet system. Toward the end of the Soviet regime, that government was often forced to grossly overstate the size of grain harvests or the preparedness of their military in order to maintain an illusion of strength and order. In other words, intelligence and facts were fixed around the policy. In essence, fixing the facts became the policy.

Self-deception was piled upon self-deception. Rather than address the systemic problems within the nation, the Soviet regime chose instead to massage the illusions until the problems became too huge to overcome. Pretending everything was fine became the chosen course of action, and the state's ability to manufacture a pleasing reality became a perfect circle of inaction and delusion. By the time the tanks rolled and the Wall fell, the deal had already gone down.

Sound familiar?

There has been a lot of noise lately in the news media about the outing of CIA agent Valerie Plame, and whether Bush advisor Karl Rove was the button-man who brought her down. Press coverage of this issue has been unexpectedly tenacious. White House spokesman Scott McClellan has been leaving his podium after press conferences lately with fresh bite marks all over his ankles and legs. The intensity of the pursuit on this issue has a lot to do with *Times* reporter Judy Miller. Like her, hate her, respect her or disdain her, but one thing is clear: The White House press corps is bird-dogging this story with alacrity because one of their own has wound up in the bucket as a result of it.

Yet even with all the coverage—the *Time* cover, the *Newsweek* cover, the growling at the press conferences, the intensity of media attention that has not even been deflected by a Supreme Court nomination—the press and far too many people seem to be letting the larger issue slide by. Reporters, columnists, and talking heads chew over minute permutations of the story like whether Rove actually said Plame's name, or whether he used her maiden name, or whether he "knowingly" did any of this. The trees are certainly interesting, but the forest deserves a lot more attention.

In short, George W. Bush and his administration are pursuing a course of determined unreality that mirrors the delusional fantasies that ultimately consigned the Soviet Union to the dustbin of history. This Rove-Plame thing is but one small aspect of the main.

Valerie Plame's career as a covert CIA operative was spent keeping weapons of mass destruction out of the hands of terrorists. Her career was destroyed by the White House because her husband, Joseph Wilson, had the gall to publicly contradict Bush and his people regarding weapons of mass destruction in Iraq. It was so important for the Bush administration to maintain the fiction that Iraq possessed these weapons that they were willing to torpedo a vital intelligence network set up to protect us all. That fiction was more important than the truth.

It seems clear that Rove was central to this action, regardless of all the arguments over the definition of "is." It is likewise becoming clear that Lewis Libby, chief of staff to Vice President Cheney, was also in on this action. However, focusing only on which laws these two may have violated in wrecking Plame's ability to do her job does not encompass the totality of the issue. Valerie Plame is not a central character in all this, but only another casualty.

George W. Bush and his people spent months telling the American public that Iraq was a direct threat to our security. They invaded based upon false pretenses. They maintain the fiction that the war was necessary when it has become manifestly clear that it was not. They maintain the fiction that freedom has been brought to Iraq when it has become manifestly clear that it has not. Perhaps worst of all, they maintain the fiction that the United States and the world are safer because of the invasion. Recent events in London rip this fantasy to shreds, not to mention the reports from the French news media that the London explosives may have been made from materials stolen from that unsecured Al-Qaqaa facility in Iraq.

A recent article from the Associated Press titled "Experts Fear Endless Terror War" noted, "An Associated Press survey of longtime students of international terrorism finds them ever more convinced, in the aftermath of London's bloody Thursday, that the world has entered a long siege in a new kind of war. They believe that al-Qaeda is mutating into a global insurgency, a possible prototype for other 21st-century movements, technologically astute, almost leaderless. And the way out is far from clear. In fact, says Michael Scheuer, the ex-CIA analyst, rather than move toward solutions, the United States took a big step backward by invading Iraq."

The article continues, "Scheuer, who headed the CIA's bin Laden unit for nine years, sees a different way out—through U.S. foreign policy. He said he resigned last November to expose the U.S. leadership's 'willful blindness' to what needs to be done: withdraw the U.S. military from the Mideast, end 'unqualified support' for Israel, sever close ties to Arab oil-state 'tyrannies.'"

Willful blindness is an appropriate phrase. It captures not only the fact that we are manufacturing threats to our security every day we remain in Iraq, but the fact that virtually everything associated with Bush administration policy depends on self-delusion and the manipulation of data to fulfill political desires. Even the most fundamental underpinnings of conservative political philosophy have been ground up in the gears of this grand fantasy.

Truth no longer matters. Ethics no longer matters. Facts are there for the twisting. Decades-old conservative ideals regarding the budget and the size of the federal government have been thrown under the bus because they are no longer convenient and get in the way of the manufacturing of reality. Soviet self-delusion led that nation into Afghanistan and disaster. The Bush administration's self-delusion has led us into Iraq.

The parallel between this Bush administration and the old, failed Soviet regime can be taken one step further. One of the main reasons the Soviet government was able to stagger on for years making up facts out of whole cloth was that the leaders of that regime were accountable to no one. The Politburo said it, and so it must be true, and if it wasn't true, there was no authority or check to their power that could blow a whistle, throw a flag, or demand an investigation. The old Soviet government lived in a bubble, free from the fear that they might be called to the carpet for lying, getting a lot of people killed, and putting the state in mortal danger.

Sound familiar? Bush and his people have managed to walk through the raindrops since 2001, managed to pull off more than a few impeachable crimes, for no other reason than that they are accountable to no one in government . . . or, more properly, because no one in government who has the power to call them to account has done so. Congress is run by Bush allies, the Justice Department is run by his longest-standing hatchet man, and all of them prefer to maintain the pleasant fictions over any attempt to fix what has gone so drastically and demonstrably wrong.

We watched the Soviets smash themselves to pieces because they refused to deal with what ailed them, because lies made life easier on the powerful, because actually attempting to address a problem might expose the powerful to censure or even removal, and because no one had the power to stop them.

It is happening again, right before our eyes.

SHORT TALES
FROM BIZARRO WORLD

19 MAY 2005

I met Saddam Hussein exactly the same number of times as Donald Rumsfeld met him. The difference is that Donald Rumsfeld met him to sell him guns, and to give him maps the better to target those guns.

George Galloway,
Respect MP for Bethnal Green and Bow, 17 May 2005

YOU KNOW things have gone more than a bit around the bend when it takes a British MP with a hard Scottish brogue to throw a little truth against the walls of the U.S. Senate chamber to see what will stick. George Galloway, accused of profiteering in the UN oil-for-food scandal, sat before Senators Coleman and Levin on Tuesday and raked America's Iraq invasion slowly and deliberately over the coals.

"I told the world that Iraq, contrary to your claims, did not have weapons of mass destruction," said Galloway. "I told the world, contrary to your claims, that Iraq had no connection to al-Qaeda. I told the world, contrary to your claims, that Iraq had no connection to the atrocity on 9/11 2001. I told the world, contrary to your claims, that the Iraqi people would resist a British and American invasion of their country and that the fall of Baghdad would not be the beginning of the end, but merely the end of the beginning. Senator, in everything I said about Iraq, I turned out to be right and you turned out to be wrong, and 100,000 people paid with their lives; 1600 of them American soldiers sent to their deaths on a pack of lies; 15,000 of them wounded, many of them disabled forever on a pack of lies."

Coleman and Levin, and anyone else listening in, must have felt like they were receiving a tongue-lashing from an angry Sean Connery. The fact that Galloway's outraged testimony went out live over the airwaves on most of the 24-hour news channels was likewise an odd twist. The American people actually saw a well-spoken contrary opinion broadcast into their homes on Tuesday, a rare event, and then watched as the talking heads scrambled to spin this square peg back into its round hole.

News about the news has been all the rage of late. In the frying pan this time around is *Newsweek*, which published a report recently from investigative journalist Michael Isikoff about American military interrogators at Guantanamo flushing a Koran down the toilet as a means of wringing information out of Muslim prisoners. The story cited an anonymous source, whose credibility and information turned out to be less than solid. The White House blamed *Newsweek* and this story for igniting riots in Afghanistan that killed fifteen people.

While it is unfortunate that *Newsweek* allowed itself to be undermined by the always-dangerous "anonymous source," the White House reaction to this has been amazing in its brazen hypocrisy. The administration has said, with solemn grief, that the reputation of the U.S. has suffered irreparable harm in the Muslim world because of *Newsweek*. Not because we invaded and occupied a Muslim nation based on false information and bald-faced lies. Not because American interrogators designed torture techniques specifically created to denigrate and humiliate anyone of Muslim faith (pantomiming homosexual sex, smearing of menstrual blood on faces, etc.). Not because innocent Iraqis were raped and murdered at Abu Ghraib. Nope, it is all because of *Newsweek* now.

In reacting to the *Newsweek* story, the White House gravely asserted its abiding respect for the Muslim faith. One wonders exactly where this newfound respect comes from, given the Abu Ghraib/ Guantanamo/invasion elephant in the room, and given the other stories that have been out there for a while now. The BBC reported in October of 2004 that Guantanamo prisoners alleged their Korans were thrown into toilets and they were ordered to abandon their faith. This harkens back to Lt. General William Boykin, Deputy Undersecretary for Defense, who did a tour of fundamentalist pulpits not long ago and spoke of the clash between Christianity and Islam. "I knew that my God was bigger than his," said Boykin. "I knew that my God was a real God and his was an idol."

Then, of course, there were those other riots. You know, the ones Jerry Falwell started back in October of 2002. In an edition of *60 Minutes* broadcast on October 6, Falwell said, "I think Mohammed was a terrorist. I read enough by both Muslims and non-Muslims, to decide that he was a violent man, a man of war." The Muslim world was outraged, and sectarian riots broke out in India that left at least eight people dead. There was no mention by the White House of Falwell destroying America's reputation.

Josh Marshall, in his TalkingPointsMemo blog, asks a pertinent question: Why is the White House involved in this *Newsweek* thing to begin with? "The White House is not a party at interest here," writes Marshall. "Perhaps the people who have been falsely accused are. Perhaps the Pentagon could demand an apology if the story turns out to be false. Or the Army. Not the White House. They are only involved here in as much as the story is bad for them politically. What I see here is an effort by the White House to set an entirely different standard when it comes to reportage that in any way reflects critically on the White House. That's dangerous and it should be recognized as such."

Perhaps the most deliciously weird aspect of all this is the White House's description of *Newsweek*'s Michael Isikoff as being motivated to write his stories by his hatred of all things Republican and all things Bush. Yet it was Isikoff's relentless pursuit of the Monica Lewinski story back in the go-go '90s that eventually led to the impeachment of President Clinton. One could argue that the impeachment was, above all other factors, the reason Bush was able to keep close enough to Gore in 2000 to let the Supremes do their thing. One wonders if Linda Tripp will be the next Clinton crusader to be thrown under the bus.

Greg Mitchell of *Editor and Publisher* frames the essential strangeness of this *Newsweek* situation perfectly. "This is an administration," writes Mitchell, "that helped sell a war on intelligence often based (as in *Newsweek*'s case) on a single source. Remember 'Curveball'? The mobile biological labs? Now McClellan reminds the media about standards that 'should be met' before running a story. Reporters at today's press briefing pressed McClellan on why he now denounces the idea of articles based on a single source when he routinely demands that they rely on just that in White House backgrounders. Or as one put it, 'it sounds like you're saying your single anonymous sources are okay and everyone else's aren't.'

"But, really," continues Mitchell, "you almost have to laugh when administration officials get all huffy about the U.S. losing respect in the Muslim world—and the fact that 'people have lost lives'— because of the nugget in *Newsweek*, when this follows Abu Ghraib, the confirmed deaths of dozens of prisoners in U.S. custody, the outsourcing of torture to Egypt and other countries, not to mention the killing of tens of thousands in Iraq in a war largely based on bogus tips from unreliable sources."

It takes an irate Scot to play the role of the dogged opposition in the U.S. Senate, and it takes a *Newsweek* article by the guy who was central to the Clinton impeachment movement to ruin America's reputation in a Muslim world reeling from invasions, torture, rape, and murder. Yes, you almost have to laugh. It's either that, or start breaking things.

DON'T LET IT
BRING YOU DOWN

WOLF BLITZER got up on his hind legs during his Sunday morning confab with Senator Biden on CNN and expressed his outrage that the Iraqi people and their so-called leaders have not thanked the United States for invading and occupying their country. "There was not one word of appreciation," said Blitzer, "to the United States for liberating Iraq from Saddam Hussein." Wolf went on to ask Biden if the Senator found this as alarming and depressing as he did.

The disconnect is staggering, the comment *so* two years ago. Remember when Dick Cheney told us before the war that, "My belief is we will, in fact, be greeted as liberators"? The vast gulf between our present reality and Cheney's pre-invasion optimism is wide enough to sail the Sixth Fleet through with room to spare. Yet there was Wolf, still waiting for the hearts and flowers.

Blitzer, one can assume, would be appalled by another video on the 'net. The video shows a caravan of oil tankers being driven by U.S. troops through Iraq. One soldier, driving the tanker and narrating the video, tells the viewer to be ready for the next stretch of road. Children, it seems, gather on that stretch of road to throw rocks at the passing soldiers. The video clearly shows young Iraqis pelting the truck as it rolls along; one rock smashes the windshield. The soldier in the video is vocally frustrated by the rules of engagement which keep him from shooting the rock-throwers.

Maybe those kids are foreign fighters, insurgents shipped in from Iran and Syria to disrupt the march of democracy.

Let's see. Tens of thousands of Iraqis have been killed and maimed during this occupation. Seventy percent of the population is unemployed. Long gas lines are the rule of the day. Hospitals don't work. Electricity is intermittent. Potable water is hard to come by. Bombs go off every day, slaying civilians, police, and soldiers indiscriminately. Iraqis disappear into torture chambers. Religious factions growl at each other like dogs in a fighting pit. The children throw rocks.

Where's the love, Wolf? Where's the thanks?

Don't let it bring you down, Wolf. It's merely an accent in the symphony. There are a number of people walking around these days groaning for a little love, for those good old days when things like rules and laws were for other people. The Abramoff scandal has a whole pile of Republican trough-diggers in Congress thinking about keeping a bail-bondsman on speed dial. It didn't used to be this way for them, and more than a few are wondering when the rug is going to get jerked out from under them.

Big George and the boys are likewise feeling the heat, and have coughed up a scattered bag of platitudes and blue-sky predictions in the form of a "plan" to "win" in Iraq. Rep. John Murtha put a burr under their collective saddle when he demanded a withdrawal from Iraq, and the White House PR mavens still haven't quite figured out how to deal with him. The old chestnuts about elitist liberal weenies don't scan with Murtha; the only time he ever stuck his pinkie finger out while drinking a latte was so he could pick up the Distinguished Service Cross he earned after a lifetime in the Marine Corps.

There is another video from Al Jazeera on the 'net allegedly showing the explosion that killed ten marines in Fallujah last week. The Pentagon folks are vehemently denying that this video actually shows those ten marines getting blown up. Perhaps they are correct, but one thing is certain. The video definitely shows a crowd of

American soldiers and a Humvee disappearing into the vortex of a terrible detonation.

Those ten marines who died last week, by the way, had names and homes. Almost half of them were not old enough to legally buy a beer in America when they died in Iraq.

Adam Kaiser was 19, and was from Naperville, Illinois. Andrew Patten was also 19, and was from Byron, Illinois. Anthony McElveen was 20, and was from Little Falls, Minnesota. Robert Martinez was also 20, and was from Splendora, Texas. Craig Watson was 21, and was from Union City, Michigan. John Holmason was also 21, and was from Scappoose, Oregon. Scott Modeen was 24, and was from Hennepin, Minnesota. David Huhn was also 24, and was from Portland, Michigan. Daniel Clay was 27, and was from Pensacola, Florida. Andy Stevens was 29, and was from Tomah, Wisconsin.

It is important to know their names, because you will never get to meet them.

Since January 2001, we have lost faith in the idea that our votes matter; we have lost two towers in New York; we have lost an entire city in Louisiana; we have lost 2,129 soldiers in Iraq; somewhere along the way we lost a whole pile of weapons of mass destruction those soldiers died trying to find; we have lost a substantial portion of our children's future by spending hundreds of billions of dollars so those soldiers could die far from home; we have lost our standing with the international community; and a good portion of the planet looks long and hard at us, wondering if we have also lost our minds.

Don't let it bring you down, though. We're staying the course, fighting them over there so we don't have to fight them here, spreading democracy, rolling with the noble cause, doing the Lord's work and saving Christmas, all at the same time. It's all good.

GEORGE AND THE AMAZING TECHNICOLOR DREAMTIE

15 APRIL 2004

THE FIRST THING you got was the tie.

You lost the importance of the press conference. You lost the fact that Bush had only done two of these prime-time gigs in his entire term, and that he hates them because he isn't good at them. You lost the fact that the 9/11 Commission had been punching him and his administration around the room for the last couple of weeks. You lost the fact that September 11 had been demystified, that the going wisdom now says it could have been stopped by an administration that was actually paying attention. You lost the fact that almost 80 American soldiers and something like 900 Iraqis had been killed in the last month of fighting, that almost 700 American soldiers have been killed since the invasion was undertaken, and that, oh by the way, there are no weapons of mass destruction in Iraq.

You lost all of that and were left with the tie around Bush's neck, the gray spotted tie that was flashing and heliographing in the camera's eye like something out of a Hunter S. Thompson fever dream, the mesmerizing swirl of reds and yellows and purples and blues that left the whole press conference behind in a hypnotizing, dazzling, inebriating swirl of flummoxed technology, and that almost certainly caused Americans from sea to shining sea to lean towards their televisions and exclaim, "Holy Christ, Marjorie, look at the man's necktie!"

But then the shock of the collision between necktie and television wore off, and you were left with the man, and his words, and certainly the most ridiculous press conference since Al Haig blithered about being in charge after Hinckley put a bullet into Ronald Reagan. They sacked Haig pretty much on the spot after that sad display. Would that the American people in the year of Our Lord 2004 could be so lucky.

Leaving aside the fact that Bush sounded for all the world like he was speaking through a mouthful of glue—and they say John Kerry is boring on the stump?—the preamble to this train wreck of a press conference is worthy of some analysis:

GWB: This has been tough weeks in that country.

WRP: Huh?

GWB: Coalition forces have encountered serious violence in some areas of Iraq.

WRP: You don't say.

GWB: In the south of Iraq, coalition forces face riots and attacks that are being incited by a radical cleric named al-Sadr.

WRP: And you know why? Because your goober proconsul Paul Bremer shut down al-Sadr's piddly little tabloid newspaper on 04 April, giving this pampered brat more street cred than he ever had before. He had plenty of people to whip into a frenzy against American forces, George, because your whole project in Iraq has been utterly devoid of meaning, direction, or even coherent planning. You went and made a martyr out of al-Sadr by closing down his newspaper, lighting a fuse that has left dozens of Americans and hundreds of Iraqis dead. Kudos, Chief.

GWB: As a proud, independent people, Iraqis do not support an indefinite occupation, and neither does America. We're not an imperial power, as nations such as Japan and Germany can attest. We're a liberating power, as nations in Europe and Asia can attest as well.

WRP: Brilliant. American military forces remain in Germany and Japan to this very day. That's not much of an object lesson. As for being a "liberating power" in Asia, I can't imagine you are referring to Vietnam, Cambodia, or Laos.

GWB: Were the coalition to step back from the June 30th pledge, many Iraqis would question our intentions and feel their hopes betrayed. And those in Iraq who trade in hatred and conspiracy theories would find a larger audience and gain a stronger hand.

WRP: I can't be sure how up on current events you are, George, but that horse pretty much left the barn.

GWB: In Fallujah, coalition forces have suspended offensive operations, allowing members of the Iraqi Governing Council and local leaders to work on the restoration of central authority in that city. These leaders are communicating with the insurgents to ensure an orderly turnover of that city to Iraqi forces, so that the resumption of military action does not become necessary.

WRP: Translation—American forces were totally shocked by the fury of the Iraqi people after this catastrophe of a military adventure, further shocked by the alliance between Shi'a and Sunni, and betrayed by ham-handed actions like Bremer's decision to shut down al-Sadr's nothing newspaper. Because the Iraqi fighters seemed perfectly capable of killing dozens of Americans at will, and because this was a political mess for you right during election season, you were forced to sue for a "cease-fire" with the people you had supposedly defeated. The result of this will be an Iraqi military opposition in Fallujah and Najaf that has had time to regroup and rearm. Congratulations. You're about to get even more people killed.

GWB: The violence we are seeing in Iraq is familiar. The terrorists who take hostages or plants a roadside bomb near Baghdad is serving the same ideology of murder that kills innocent people on trains in Madrid, and murders children on buses in Jerusalem, and blows up a nightclub in Bali and cuts the throat of a young reporter for being a Jew. We've seen the same ideology of murder in the killing of 241 Marines in Beirut, the first attack on the World Trade Center, in the destruction of two embassies in Africa, in the attack on the USS *Cole,* and in the merciless horror inflicted upon thousands of innocent men and women and children on September the 11th, 2001.

WRP: Two problems, one of which is the same grammar catastrophe you appear incapable of avoiding. You say "The terrorists who . . . is serving . . ." Come on, George. "The terrorists who . . . are serving . . ." is the way to work that English language. Make it yours, George. Abandon "Nooo-kyooo-lurr" as an actual word; it isn't one. Beyond that, the fact that you have again connected Iraq to September 11—and, boy, Beirut was just out of nowhere—is shameful and disgraceful. Just stop.

GWB: The terrorists have lost the shelter of the Taliban and the training camps in Afghanistan. They have lost safe havens in Pakistan.

WRP: Um, no. Because you took the best troops out of Afghanistan and threw them into Iraq, the Taliban and al Qaeda are pretty much running around free there again. They have free and open access to Pakistan for the same reason. I hear the heroin crop in Afghanistan this year is going to be simply divine, which works in your favor if you think about it. After all, what fun is a severe economic downturn if there isn't cheap access to good smack?

GWB: They lost an ally in Baghdad.

WRP: They never had an ally in Baghdad. Again, this allegation has been disproved more times than Piltdown man. You need to get some new material, George. I suggest invading France immediately. It's not like those cheese-eating surrender monkeys were dead-bang right about this invasion being a disaster in the making.

A good military stomping will shut them up, and you can bring back the freedom fries fad.

GWB: We will succeed in Iraq. We're carrying out a decision that has already been made and will not change.

WRP: Yup, you made the decision the day you showed up in Washington with your band of neocon Vulcans. Never let pesky things like facts get in the way of a decision that has already been made.

That's about as much of that as anyone could stand. My mother had called me by this point screaming, "This is a President? I feel like I want to cry!" I had to break it to her that the worst was yet to come. The press were about to get their shot. Seldom in human history have so many pointed questions gone so amazingly unanswered. Some examples, which speak for themselves:

QUESTION: Mr. President, before the war, you and members of your administration made several claims about Iraq: that U.S. troops would be greeted as liberators with sweets and flowers; that Iraqi oil revenue would pay for most of the reconstruction; and that Iraq not only had weapons of mass destruction but, as Secretary of Defense Rumsfeld said, we know where they are. How do you explain to Americans how you got that so wrong? And how do you answer your opponents who say that you took this nation to war on the basis of what have turned out to be a series of false premises?

GWB: Well, let me step back and review my thinking prior to going into Iraq. First, the lesson of September the 11th is that when this nation sees a threat, a gathering threat, we got to deal with it. We can no longer hope that oceans protect us from harm. Every threat we must take seriously. Saddam Hussein was a threat. He was a threat because he had used weapons of mass destruction on his own people. He was a threat because he coddled terrorists. He was a threat because he funded suiciders. He was a threat to the region. He was a threat to the United States.

And we've been there a year. I know that seems like a long time. It seems like a long time to the loved ones whose troops have been overseas. But when you think about where the country has come from, it's a relatively short period of time. And we're making progress. There's no question it's been a tough, tough series of weeks for the American people. It's been really tough for the families. I understand that. It's been tough on this administration. But we're doing the right thing. And as to whether or not I made decisions based upon polls, I don't. I just don't make decisions that way. I fully understand the consequences of what we're doing. We're changing the world, and the world will be better off and America will be more secure as a result of the actions we're taking.

WRP: Ooooookay . . . raise your hand if you see an answer in there? "Suiciders?" There are no weapons of mass destruction, despite the fact that Rumsfeld said he knew where they were—and it bears mention that Bush referred to Rumsfeld in his preamble as the Secretary of State. We were hardly welcomed as liberators, and the oil infrastructure is in total disarray. No answers from George. And as far as "We're changing the world" goes, George, there's an old saying: Any jackass can knock down a barn. You change the barn when you smash it, but not many people would label it an improvement. Good thing your triumphalist streak is under control, though.

Moving on:

QUESTION: Mr. President, why are you and the vice president insisting on appearing together before the 9/11 commission? And, Mr. President, who will we be handing the Iraqi government over to on June 30th?

GWB: We'll find that out soon. That's what Mr. Brahimi is doing. He's figuring out the nature of the entity we'll be handing sovereignty over. And, secondly, because the 9/11 Commission wants to ask us questions, that's why we're meeting. And I look forward to meeting with them and answering their questions.

FOLLOW-UP: I was asking why you're appearing together, rather than separately, which was their request.

GWB: Because it's a good chance for both of us to answer questions that the 9/11 Commission is looking forward to asking us. And I'm looking forward to answering them.

WRP: The talking heads before this press conference were saying it was absolutely, positively vital for Bush to deliver some sort of coherent plan for the immediate future of Iraq, including the hand-over. Here was a perfect opportunity to explain that plan, and George punted. You'll know when I know, hyuk hyuk hyuk. As for the whole thing about Bush and Cheney appearing together, the answer is pretty plain. George doesn't know much of anything about how his administration is being run, as was made horrifyingly clear in this event. Dick needs to be there to work the strings. The 9/11 Commission couldn't do much with "I love America, I love freedom, I love America, freedom, America, democracy, pzzzzcheeeeezzzz . . ." That's about all Bush could give them without a wingman.

Moving on:

QUESTION: In the last campaign, you were asked a question about the biggest mistake you'd made in your life, and you used to like to joke that it was trading Sammy Sosa. You've looked back before 9-11 for what mistakes might have been made. After 9-11, what would your biggest mistake be, would you say, and what lessons have you learned from it?

GWB: I wish you'd have given me this written question ahead of time so I could plan for it. John, I'm sure historians will look back and say, gosh, he could've done it better this way or that way. You know, I just—I'm sure something will pop into my head here in the midst of this press conference, with all the pressure of trying to come up with answer, but it hadn't yet. I would've gone into Afghanistan the way we went into Afghanistan. Even knowing what I know today about the stockpiles of weapons, I still would've called upon the world to deal with Saddam Hussein. See, I'm of the belief that we'll find out the truth on the weapons. That's why we sent up the independent commission. I look forward to hearing the truth as to exactly where they are. They could still be there. They could be hidden, like the 50 tons of mustard gas in a turkey farm.

One of the things that Charlie Duelfer talked about was that he was surprised of the level of intimidation he found amongst people who should know about weapons and their fear of talking about them because they don't want to be killed. You know, there's this kind of—there's a terror still in the soul of some of the people in Iraq. They're worried about getting killed, and therefore they're not going to talk. But it'll all settle out, John. We'll find out the truth about the weapons at some point in time. However, the fact that he had the capacity to make them bothers me today just like it would have bothered me then. He's a dangerous man. He's a man who actually not only had weapons of mass destruction—the reason I can say that with certainty is because he used them. And I have no doubt in my mind that he would like to have inflicted harm, or paid people to inflict harm, or trained people to inflict harm, on America, because he hated us. I hope—I don't want to sound like I have made no mistakes. I'm confident I have. I just haven't—you just put me under the spot here, and maybe I'm not as quick on my feet as I should be in coming up with one.

WRP: So much of this question and answer sums up the entire issue that squats incoherently before the American people, and never mind the tacit admission that he is helpless if he doesn't get the questions beforehand. Even Nixon admitted making mistakes.

Have you made any mistakes, George? The Towers came down; the Taliban and al Qaeda are back in force in Afghanistan; there are about 700 dead American soldiers and well over 10,000 dead Iraqis in the Middle East; there are no weapons of mass destruction in Iraq; they had nothing to do with September 11; Osama bin Laden has been given this great gift because we invaded a Muslim country on a non-existent pretext, and by the way we failed to catch the guy "Dead or Alive"; we have manufactured thousands more terrorists with this invasion; the budget is annihilated; the Homeland Security Department is a total boondoggle . . . Nope, I can't think of any mistakes. By the way, the Iraqi WMDs are hidden at a turkey farm. Pass it on.

The tie only worked for a minute. After that, the only thing hypnotizing on the television was this small fraction of a man playing at being Presidential while the world crashes down around his ears.

God help us all.

THE WAR IS LOST

WE HAVE TRAVELED a long, dark, strange road since the attacks of September 11. We have all suffered, we have all known fear and anger, and sometimes hatred. Many of us have felt—probably more than we are willing to admit it—at one time or another a desire for revenge, so deep was the wound inflicted upon us during that wretched, unforgettable Tuesday morning in September of 2001.

But we have come now to the end of a week so awful, so terrible, so wrenching that the most basic moral fabric of that which we believe is good and great—the basic moral fabric of the United States of America—has been torn bitterly asunder.

We are awash in photographs of Iraqi men—not terrorists, just people—lying in heaps on cold floors with leashes around their necks. We are awash in photographs of men chained so remorselessly that their backs are arched in agony, men forced to masturbate for cameras, men forced to pretend to have sex with one another for cameras, men forced to endure attacks from dogs, men with electrodes attached to them as they stand, hooded, in fear of their lives.

The worst, amazingly, is yet to come. A new battery of photographs and videotapes, as yet unreleased, awaits over the horizon of our abused understanding. These photos and videos, also from the Abu Ghraib prison, are reported to show U.S. soldiers gang raping an

Iraqi woman, U.S. soldiers beating an Iraqi man nearly to death, U.S. troops posing, smirks affixed, with decomposing Iraqi bodies, and Iraqi troops under U.S. command raping young boys.

George W. Bush would have us believe that these horrors were restricted to a sadistic few, and would have us believe that these horrors happened only in Abu Ghraib. Yet reports are surfacing now of similar treatment at another U.S. detention center in Iraq called Camp Bucca. According to these reports, Iraqi prisoners in Camp Bucca were beaten, humiliated, hogtied, and had scorpions placed on their naked bodies.

In the eyes of the world, this is America today. It cannot be dismissed as an anomaly because it went on and on and on in the Abu Ghraib prison, and because now we hear of Camp Bucca. According to the British press, there are some 30 other cases of torture and humiliation under investigation. The Bush administration went out of its way to cover up this disgrace, declaring secret the Army report on these atrocities. That, pointedly, is against the rules and against the law. You can't call something classified just because it is embarrassing and disgusting. It was secret, but now it is out, and the whole world has been shown the dark, scabrous underbelly of Bush's definition of freedom.

The beginnings of actual political fallout began to find their way into the White House last week. Representative John Murtha of Pennsylvania, the House Democrats' most vocal defense hawk, joined Minority Leader Nancy Pelosi to declare that the conflict is "unwinnable." Murtha, a Vietnam veteran, rocked the Democratic caucus when he said at a leaders' luncheon Tuesday that the United States cannot win the war in Iraq.

"Unwinnable." Well, it only took about fourteen months.

Also last week, calls for the resignation of Defense Secretary Don Rumsfeld became strident. Pelosi accused Rumsfeld of being "in denial about Iraq," and said U.S. soldiers "are suffering great casualties and injuries, and American taxpayers are paying an enormous price" because Rumsfeld "has done a poor job as secretary of defense." Representative Charlie Rangel, a leading critic of the Iraq invasion, has filed articles of impeachment against Rumsfeld.

So there's the heat. But let us consider the broader picture here in the context of that one huge word: "Unwinnable." Why did we do this in the first place? There have been several reasons offered over the last sixteen months for why we needed to do this thing.

It started, for real, in January 2003 when George W. Bush said in his State of the Union speech that Iraq was in possession of 26,000 liters of anthrax, 38,000 liters of botulinum toxin, 500 tons of sarin, mustard, and VX, 30,000 munitions to deliver this stuff, and that Iraq was seeking uranium from Niger to build nuclear bombs.

That reason has been scratched off the list because, as has been made painfully clear now, there are no such weapons in Iraq. The Niger claim, in particular, has caused massive embarrassment for America because it was so farcical, and has led to a federal investigation of this White House because two administration officials took revenge upon Joseph Wilson's wife for Wilson's exposure of the lie.

Next on the list was September 11, and the oft-repeated accusation that Saddam Hussein must have been at least partially responsible. That one collapsed as well—Bush himself had to come out and say Saddam had nothing to do with it.

Two reasons down, so the third must be freedom and liberty for the Iraqi people. Once again, however, facts interfere. America does not want a democratic Iraq, because a democratic Iraq would quickly become a Shi'ite fundamentalist Iraq allied with the Shi'ite fundamentalist nation of Iran, a strategic situation nobody with a brain wants to see come to pass. It has been made clear by Paul Bremer, the American administrator of Iraq, that whatever the new Iraqi government comes to look like, it will have no power to make any laws of any kind, it will have no control over the security of Iraq, and it will have no power over the foreign troops that occupy its soil. This is, perhaps, some bizarre new definition of democracy not yet in the dictionary, but it is not democracy by any currently accepted definition I have ever heard of.

So . . . the reason to go to war because of weapons of mass destruction is destroyed. The reason to go to war because of connections to September 11 is destroyed. The reason to go to war in order to bring freedom and democracy to Iraq is destroyed. What is left? The one reason left has been unfailingly flapped around by defenders of this administration and supporters of this war: Saddam Hussein was a terrible, terrible man. He killed his own people. He tortured his own people. The Iraqis are better off without him, and so the war is justified.

And here, now, is the final excuse destroyed. We have killed more than 10,000 innocent Iraqi civilians in this invasion, and maimed countless others. The photos from Abu Ghraib prison show that we, like Saddam Hussein, torture and humiliate the Iraqi people. Worst of all, we do this in the same prison Hussein used to do his torturing. The "rape rooms," often touted by Bush as justification for the invasion, are back. We are the killers now. We are the torturers now. We have achieved moral equivalence with the Butcher of Baghdad.

This war is lost. I mean not just the Iraq war, but George W. Bush's ridiculous "War on Terror" as a whole. I say ridiculous because this "War on Terror" was never, ever something we were going to win. What began on September 11 with the world wrapping us in its loving embrace has collapsed today in a literal orgy of shame and disgrace.

We saw a prime example of this during Friday's farce of a Senate hearing into the Abu Ghraib disaster, which starred Don Rumsfeld. From his bully pulpit spoke Senator Joe Lieberman, who parrots the worst of Bush's war propaganda with unfailingly dreary regularity. Responding to the issue of whether or not Bush and Rumsfeld should apologize for Abu Ghraib, Lieberman stated that none of the terrorists had apologized for September 11.

There it was, in a nutshell. There was the idea, oft promulgated by the administration, that September 11 made any barbarism, any extreme, any horror brought forth by the United States acceptable, and even desirable. There was the institutionalization of revenge as a basis for policy. Sure, Abu Ghraib was bad, Mr. Lieberman put forth. But September 11 happened, so all bets are off.

Thus fails the "War on Terror." September 11 did not demand of us the lowest common denominator, did not demand of us that we become that which we despise and denounce. September 11 demanded that we be better, greater, more righteous than those who brought death to us. September 11 demanded that we be better, and in doing so, we would show the world that those who attacked us are far, far less than we are. That would have been victory, with nary a shot being fired.

Our leaders, however, took us in exactly the opposite direction.

Every reason to go to Iraq has failed to retain even a semblance of credibility. Every bit of propaganda Osama bin Laden served up to the Muslim world for why America should be attacked and destroyed has been given credibility by what has taken place in Iraq. Victory in this "War on Terror," a propaganda war from the beginning, has been given to the September 11 attackers by the hand of George W. Bush, and by the hand of those who enabled his incomprehensible blundering.

The war is lost.

ATTACK ON IRAN:
A LOOMING FOLLY

09 JANUARY 2006

THE WIRES have been humming since before the New Year with reports that the Bush administration is planning an attack on Iran. "The Bush administration is preparing its NATO allies for a possible military strike against suspected nuclear sites in Iran in the New Year, according to German media reports, reinforcing similar earlier suggestions in the Turkish media," reported UPI on 30 December.

"The Berlin daily *Der Tagesspiegel* this week," continued UPI, "quoted 'NATO intelligence sources' who claimed that the NATO allies had been informed that the United States is currently investigating all possibilities of bringing the mullah-led regime into line, including military options. This 'all options are open' line has been President George W. Bush's publicly stated policy throughout the past 18 months."

An examination of the ramifications of such an attack is desperately in order.

1. BLOWBACK IN IRAQ

The recent elections in Iraq were dominated by an amalgam of religiously fundamentalist Shi'ite organizations, principally the Dawa Party and the Supreme Council for Islamic Revolution in Iraq (SCIRI). Both Dawa and SCIRI have umbilical connections to the fundamentalist Shi'ite leadership in Iran that go back decades. In essence, Iran now owns a significant portion of the Iraqi government.

Should the United States undertake military action against Iran, the ramifications in Iraq would be immediate and extreme.

In the first eight days of January, eighteen U.S. troops have been killed in Iraq, compounded by another twelve deaths from a Blackhawk helicopter crash on Saturday. Much of the violence aimed at American forces is coming from disgruntled Sunni factions who have their own militias, who believe the last elections were a sham, and who hold little political power in the government.

If the U.S. attacks Iran, it is probable that American forces—already taxed by attacks from Sunni factions—will also face reprisal attacks in Iraq from Shi'ite factions loyal to Iran. The result will be a dramatic escalation in U.S. and civilian casualties, and U.S. forces will be required to bunker themselves further into their bases to fight the very government they just finished helping into power. Iraq, already a seething cauldron, will sink further into chaos.

2. IRAN'S ARMAMENTS

Unlike Iraq, Iran has not spent the last fifteen years having its conventional forces worn down by grueling sanctions, repeated attacks, and two American-led wars. While Iran's conventional army is not what it was during the heyday of the Iran-Iraq war—their armaments have deteriorated and the veterans of that last war have retired—the nation enjoys substantial military strength nonetheless.

According to a report issued by the Center for Strategic and International Studies in December of 2004, Iran "has some 540,000 men under arms and over 350,000 reserves. They include 120,000 Iranian Revolutionary Guards trained for land and naval asymmetrical warfare. Iran's military also includes holdings of 1,613 main battle tanks, 21,600 other armored fighting vehicles, 3,200 artillery weapons, 306 combat aircraft, 60 attack helicopters, 3 submarines, 59 surface combatants, and 10 amphibious ships.

"Iran is now the only regional military power that poses a significant conventional military threat to Gulf stability," continued the CSIS report. "Iran has significant capabilities for asymmetric warfare, and poses the additional threat of proliferation. There is considerable evidence that it is developing both a long-range missile force and a range of weapons of mass destruction. It has never properly declared its holdings of chemical weapons, and the status of its biological weapons programs is unknown."

A MILNET (the open source military information database) brief issued in February 2005 reports, "Due to its position astride the Persian Gulf, Iran has constantly been a threat to the Gulf. The so called 'Tanker' wars in the late 1980s put Iran squarely in the bullseye of all nations seeking to transport oil out of the region. Even the small navy that Iran puts to sea is capable enough to harass shipping, and several cases of small boat operations against oil well heads in the Gulf during that period made it clear small asymmetrical tactics of the Iranian Navy could be quite effective.

"More concerning," continued the MILNET brief, "is the priority placed on expanding and modernizing its Navy. The CSIS report cites numerous areas where Iran has funded modernization including the most troublesome aspect, anti-shipping cruise missiles: 'Iran has obtained new anti-ship missiles and missile patrol craft from China, midget submarines from North Korea, submarines from Russia, and modern mines.'"

It is Iran's missile armaments that pose the greatest concern for American forces in the Gulf, especially for the U.S. Navy. Iran's coast facing the Persian Gulf is a looming wall of mountains that look down upon any naval forces arrayed in those waters. The Gulf itself only has one exit, the Strait of Hormuz, which is also dominated by the mountainous Iranian coastline. In essence, Iran holds the high ground in the Gulf. Missile batteries arrayed in those mountains could raise bloody havoc with any fleet deployed below.

Of all the missiles in Iran's armament, the most dangerous is the Russian-made SS-N-22 Sunburn. These missiles are, simply, the fastest anti-ship weapons on the planet. The Sunburn can reach Mach 3 at high altitude. Its maximum low-altitude speed is Mach 2.2, some three times faster than the American-made Harpoon. The Sunburn takes two short minutes to cover its full range. The missile's manufacturers state that one or two missiles could cripple a destroyer, and five missiles could sink a 20,000 ton ship. The Sunburn is also superior to the Exocet missile. Recall that it was two Exocets that ripped the USS *Stark* to shreds in 1987, killing 37 sailors. The *Stark* could not see them to stop them.

The U.S. aircraft carrier *Theodore Roosevelt* is currently deployed in the Persian Gulf, with some 7,000 souls aboard. Sailing with the *Roosevelt* is the Tarawa Expeditionary Strike Force, which includes the USS *Tarawa*, the USS *Austin,* and the USS *Pearl Harbor.* The Sunburn missile, with its incredible speed and ability to avoid radar detection, would do terrible damage to these ships if Iran chose to retaliate in the Gulf after an American attack within its borders.

Beyond the naval threat is the possibility of Iran throwing its military muscle into the ongoing struggle in Iraq. Currently, the U.S. is facing an asymmetrical attack from groups wielding small arms, shoulder-fired grenades, and roadside bombs. The vaunted American military has suffered 2,210 deaths and tens of thousands of wounded from this form of warfare. The occupation of Iraq has become a guerilla war, a siege that has lasted more than a thousand days. If Iran decides to throw any or all of its 23,000 armored fighting vehicles, along with any or all of its nearly million-strong army, into the Iraq fray, the situation in the Middle East could become unspeakably dire.

3. THE SYRIAN CONNECTION

In February of 2005, Iran and Syria agreed upon a mutual protection pact to combat "challenges and threats" in the region. This was a specific reaction to the American invasion of Iraq, and a reaction to America's condemnation of Syria after the death of Lebanese Prime

Minister Rafik Hariri, which was widely seen as an assassination ordered from Damascus. An attack on Iran would trigger this mutual defense pact, and could conceivably bring Syria into direct conflict with American forces.

Like Iran, Syria's military is nothing to scoff at. Virtually every credible analysis has Syria standing as the strongest military force in the Middle East after Israel. Damascus has been intent for years upon establishing significant military strength to serve as a counterweight to Israel's overwhelming capabilities. As of 2002, Syria had some 215,000 soldiers under arms, 4,700 tanks, and a massive artillery capability. The Syrian Air Force is made up of ten to eleven fighter/attack squadrons and sixteen fighter squadrons, totaling somewhere near 650 aircraft.

Syria also possesses one of the largest arsenals of ballistic missiles in the region, comprised primarily of SCUD-derived systems. Iran, North Korea, and China have been willing providers of state-of-the-art technologies. Compounding this is the well-based suspicion that Syria has perhaps the most advanced chemical weapons capability in the Persian Gulf.

4. CHINA AND THE U.S. ECONOMY

While the ominous possibilities of heightened Iraqi chaos, missiles in the Gulf, and Syrian involvement loom large if the U.S. attacks Iran, all pale in comparison to the involvement of China in any U.S./Iran engagement.

China's economy is exploding, hampered only by their great thirst for petroleum and natural gas to fuel their industry. In the last several months, China has inked deals with Iran for $70 billion worth of Iranian oil and natural gas. China will purchase 250 million tons of liquefied natural gas from Iran over the next 30 years, will develop the massive Yadavaran oil field in Iran, and will receive 150,000 barrels of oil per day from that field. China is seeking the construction of a pipeline from Iran to the Caspian Sea, where it would link with another planned pipeline running from Kazakhstan to China.

Any U.S. attack on Iran could be perceived by China as a direct threat to its economic health. Further, any fighting in the Persian Gulf would imperil the tankers running China's liquefied natural gas through the Strait of Hormuz. Should China decide to retaliate against the U.S. to defend its oil and natural gas deal with Iran, the U.S. would be faced with a significant threat. This threat exists not merely on a military level, though China could force a confrontation in the Pacific by way of Taiwan. More significantly, China holds a large portion of the American economy in the palm of its hand.

Paul Craig Roberts, writing for the *American Conservative,* said in July of 2005 that "As a result of many years of persistent trade surpluses with the United States, the Japanese government holds dollar reserves of approximately $1 trillion. China's accumulation of dollars is approximately $600 billion. South Korea holds about $200 billion. These sums give these countries enormous leverage over the United States. By dumping some portion of their reserves, these countries could put the dollar under intense pressure and send U.S. interest rates skyrocketing. Washington would really have to anger Japan and Korea to provoke such action, but in a showdown with China—over Taiwan, for example—China holds the cards. China and Japan, and the world at large, have more dollar reserves than they require. They would have no problem teaching a hegemonic superpower a lesson if the need arose.

"The hardest blow on Americans," concluded Roberts, "will fall when China does revalue its currency. When China's currency ceases to be undervalued, American shoppers in Wal-Mart, where 70% of the goods on the shelves are made in China, will think they are in Neiman Marcus. Price increases will cause a dramatic reduction in American real incomes. If this coincides with rising interest rates and a setback in the housing market, American consumers will experience the hardest times since the Great Depression."

In short, China has the American economy by the throat. Should they decide to squeeze, we will all feel it. Their strong hand in this even extends to the diplomatic realm; China is a permanent member of the United Nations Security Council, and could veto any actions against Iran proposed by the United States.

5. AMERICAN PREPAREDNESS

American citizens have for decades taken it as a given that our military can overwhelm and overcome any foe on the battlefield. The rapid victory during the first Gulf War cemented this perception. The last three years of the Iraq occupation, however, have sapped this confidence. Worse, the occupation has done great damage to the strength of the American military, justifying the decrease in confidence. Thanks to repeated deployments to Iraq and Afghanistan, recruiting is at an all-time low. Soldiers with vital training and know-how are refusing to re-enlist. Across the board, the American military is stretched to the breaking point.

Two vaunted economists—one a Nobel-Prize winner and the other a nationally renowned budget expert—have analyzed the data at hand and put a price tag on the Iraq occupation. According to Linda Bilmes of Harvard and Nobel Laureate Joseph E. Stiglitz of Columbia University, the final cost of the Iraq occupation will run between $1 trillion and $2 trillion, surpassing by orders of magnitude the estimates put forth by the Bush administration. If an engagement with Iran envelops our forces in Iraq, and comes to involve Syria, our economy will likely shatter under the strain of fighting so many countries simultaneously. Add to this the economic threat posed by China and the economic threat implicit in any substantial disruption of the distribution of Mideast petroleum to the globe.

If Iran and Syria—with their significant armaments, missile technologies, and suspected chemical weapons capabilities—decide to engage with the relatively undersized U.S. force in Iraq, our troops there will be fish in a barrel. Iran's position over the Gulf would make resupply by ship and air support from carriers a dangerous affair. In the worst-case scenario, the newly minted American order of battle requiring the use of nuclear weapons to rescue a surrounded and imperiled force could come into play, hurling the entire planet into military and diplomatic bedlam.

CONCLUSION: IS ANY OF THIS POSSIBLE?

The question must be put as directly as possible: What manner of maniac would undertake a path so fraught with peril and potential economic catastrophe? It is difficult to imagine a justification for any action that could envelop the United States in a military and economic conflict with Iraq, Iran, Syria, and China simultaneously.

Iran is suspected by many nations of working towards the development of nuclear weapons, but even this justification has been tossed into a cocked hat. Recently, Russian President Vladimir Putin bluntly stated that Iran is not developing its nuclear capability for any reasons beyond peaceful energy creation, and pledged to continue assisting Iran in this endeavor. Therefore, any attack upon Iran's nuclear facilities will bring Russia into the mess. Iran also stands accused of aiding terrorism across the globe. The dangers implicit in any attack upon that nation, however, seem to significantly offset whatever gains could be made in the so-called "War on Terror."

Unfortunately, all the dangers in the world are no match for the self-assurance of a bubble-encased zealot. What manner of maniac would undertake such a dangerous course? Look no further than 1600 Pennsylvania Avenue.

George W. Bush and his administration have consistently undertaken incredibly dangerous courses of action in order to garner political power on the home front. Recall the multiple terror threats lobbed out by the administration whenever damaging political news appeared in the media. More significantly, recall Iraq. Karl Rove, Bush's most senior advisor, notoriously told Republicans on the ballot during the 2002 midterms to "run on the war." The invasion of

Iraq provided marvelous political cover for the GOP not only during those midterms, but during the 2004 Presidential election.

What kind of political cover would be gained from an attack on Iran, and from the diversion of attention to that attack? The answer lies in one now-familiar name: Jack Abramoff. The Abramoff scandal threatens to subsume all the hard-fought GOP gains in Congress, and the 2006 midterms are less than a year away.

Is any of this a probability? Logic says no, but logic seldom plays any part in modern American politics. All arguments that the Bush administration would be insane to attack Iran and risk a global conflagration for the sake of political cover run into one unavoidable truth.

They did it once already in Iraq.

THE PROPHECY OF OIL

07 MARCH 2005

ON 27 AUGUST 1859, Edwin Drake's oil well in Titusville, Pennsylvania, struck a gusher, making him the man credited with drilling the first commercially successful oil well in America. In the time between then and now, the world has burned through about 900 billion barrels of Drake's discovery.

Global daily oil consumption today stands at around 82 million barrels, and many experts believe the emerging mega-industrialization of nations like China and India will cause that daily consumption to reach at least 120 million barrels a day by the year 2030. Not to fear, however: ExxonMobil believes there are some 14 trillion barrels still in the ground, including non-conventional resource fields like the tar sands of Canada and petroleum-rich shale in the western United States.

In the last several years, a theory known as "Peak Oil" has been working its way into the mainstream. Chief proponent of this theory is Dr. Colin Campbell, a retired oil-industry geologist now living in Ireland. Dr. Campbell, who has been raising warnings about Peak Oil for some fifteen years, believes that global consumption of oil is surpassing not only the amount of oil being pulled from the ground, not only the amount of oil left to be found, but also the ability of technology to compensate for what he sees as an inevitable and looming shortfall.

The "peak," believes Campbell, will come as early as next year, heralding a steady rise in prices and the end of cheap oil as we have known it, causing a seismic shock within the global economy. "The perception of this decline changes the entire world we know," said Dr. Campbell in a September 2004 report from the *Wall Street Journal.* "Up till now we've been living in a world with the assumption of growth driven by oil. Now we have to face the other side of the mountain."

The oil industry, predictably, considers Campbell to be a doomsaying loony, an espouser of flat-earth economics who totally discounts both the vast amounts of oil yet to be drilled, and the ability of technology to find more. Their argument is not without merit, as claims that the petroleum paradigm is on the edge of extinction are as old as the industry itself.

Sixteen years after Drake's well struck oil, for example, Pennsylvania's chief geologist warned it would soon run out. Clearly, this was not the case. Campbell himself has not helped his credibility; the expected date of imminent catastrophe quoted by the doctor has been pushed back with regularity since 1990 as each non-disastrous year passes with the industry still intact.

More and more, however, noted energy analysts are coming to heed Campbell's warnings. The respected Washington-based consulting firm PFC Energy published a report endorsing his theory, noting that the exact date of the catastrophe is less important than the fact that it is coming. PFC was hesitant at first to hang its hat on Dr. Campbell, but came to the conclusion that the decline in global oil discoveries has become so dramatic that it cannot be ignored, and that this decline calls into question whether technology can save the industry before the clock winds down to zero.

Ultimately, the debate over whether "Peak Oil" is a looming reality or merely Chicken-Littlism is wide of the point the planet must come to address. Posit for the moment that ExxonMobil and the rest of the petroleum industry are correct in their belief that trillions of barrels of oil await discovery and drilling, and that the petroleum paradigm is safe and secure for centuries to come. Even if this assumption is true, the fact remains that the paradigm itself is a suicide ride leading ever downward to danger and, ultimately, disaster.

No one can question the benefits oil has brought to global society. Here in America, millions of homes are heated with oil. Millions of cars make it easier for millions of people to get to work and take care of their business. Millions of trucks and ships have delivered billions of tons of produce to all points on the compass; one could argue that the defining truth of the luxury inherent in Western society is the ability to stand in a snow bank in Maine and enjoy a fresh pineapple from Hawaii.

Millions of people can get from New York to Los Angeles in a day, thanks to airplanes. The incomes and livelihoods of millions—workers in industry and agriculture and transportation and food services to name a few—depend upon oil. All of these benefits, all of these achievements, along with countless others, come from the drilling and processing of petroleum. Oil infuses virtually every aspect of our civilization. It is the basis of the global economy. It is the inescapable ingredient that creates, supports, and sustains the world as we know it.

Yet even as oil gives generously with one hand, it takes grievously with the other. If the petroleum industry is correct and there remain trillions of barrels to be plumbed, that oil is located for the most part in some of the most dangerous and unstable places on the planet. That danger and instability has been created, in no small part, by the fact that oil can be found there.

Oil revenues fund global terrorism. Oil resources motivate wars, and more wars, and more wars. This is the sharp other edge of the sword; if the petroleum industry is correct and oil can be found and drilled for generations to come, that means generations to come will be required to share the death and destruction we endure today in the grubbing for oil. There is no escaping this.

Oil is dirty, and its byproducts are doing demonstrable and ever-increasing damage to the environment that sustains life on Earth.

Thanks to tanker spills, dumping, and the inevitable leakage of petroleum byproducts from the global shipping industry, every centimeter of ocean on the planet is covered by a microscopically thin skim of oil.

All of the scooters, motorcycles, cars, trucks, buses, airplanes, tanks, troop transports, and other oil-fueled vehicles are releasing dramatic levels of poison into the atmosphere every minute of every day, with no letup in sight. This is chewing inexorably into planetary stability, melting the ice caps and blowing vast holes in the ozone. The "junk-science" claims of those defending the paradigm are growing ever thinner, much like the icebergs in Greenland.

Finally, and most importantly, our planetary addiction to oil, combined with the incomprehensibly huge profits to be made from the development and sale of oil, have led to the establishment of political and economic power combines that are as dominant as petroleum itself. Governments all around the world, most notably here in America but also in places like Saudi Arabia, China, and Russia, are either beholden to petroleum power combines or controlled outright by them.

When Vice President Dick Cheney, himself a creation of petroleum combines, memorably stated that it is the God-given right of every American to consume as much cheap gas as they can while driving the largest SUVs they can find, he was speaking the gospel of ascendant power. Neither reasonable argument nor empirical data can shake the faithful from this premise.

So long as there is oil and trillions of dollars to be made from it, this gospel will continue to be preached even as all the attendant problems of oil attack the basic underpinnings of life and liberty. The paradigm will be continued by any means necessary so long as the ones made powerful by it reign supreme. This begets a cycle of violence, pollution, corruption, greed, and ever-increasing power for the few over the many that has nowhere to go but, inevitably, down.

Only a maniac would hope for the immediate collapse of the petroleum paradigm and the social, economic, and military chaos that would ensue. If all the oil in the world disappeared tomorrow morning, millions of people would be dead by sundown, and billions more would follow soon after into the grave. All of modern agriculture is fully dependent on petroleum. None but the purest of psychopaths would look forward to a catastrophe of this magnitude.

Something, however, must be done. If the "Peak Oil" theory is an accurate prediction of the imminent future, something must be done. If "Peak Oil" is only a myth, something must still be done. One way or the other, this paradigm is going to destroy itself, and it will take a monstrous number of people with it.

If the powerful few who control the reins of our oil-dependent world are smart, they will invest a considerable chunk of their profits into a crash program to develop a new, sustainable source of energy. This program must dwarf the Manhattan Project in scope, funding, and immediacy. Human ingenuity is boundless, and something like cold fusion merely awaits the desire and effort to find it and make it functional.

Those addicted to the power and profits given them by oil can patent this new energy source and slowly but surely use it to supplant petroleum as the dominant truth of the planet. The power and the profits will be there for them in this, and the overhead required to locate, process, and distribute oil while killing anyone who might disrupt the flow will cease to exist.

Along the way, the air and water we need will lose their gritty, metallic taste. In other words, nothing will change and everything will change. While many will be justifiably outraged by an argument that essentially advocates for the powerful to remain powerful, few other options that do not include a global catastrophe appear to be on the table, and the clock is running.

Will this happen in time? Will it happen at all? It is, unfortunately, doubtful. Among other reasons the powerful have for maintaining this smoggy status quo is the attendant profits to be made from waging wars over oil. The war-making business is a trillion-dollar global industry. If technology were introduced that rendered oil obsolete, the deep well of cash to be made by arming and training armies would become a dry hole.

If a metaphor is needed to cement the final destination of this paradigm, consider again Edwin Drake, who got this ball rolling 146 years ago. Despite being the man to "discover" petroleum, despite being the father of what grew into a fabulously rich industry, Drake himself went broke as a result of his overextended speculation. He died in 1880, a penniless old man.

In Drake we find the prophecy of oil, a resource that gives much but takes more, a recourse that will leave us all sooner or later holding our empty hands up to an empty sky.

ONE FOR ALL

WHEN I WAS TEN years old, a man attempted suicide by fire in the front seat of my mother's car. Back then it was me and mom and the cats in a house near Boston College. She was putting herself through law school at night while working various jobs by day, and while we weren't rolling in material possessions by any means, that car of hers was the other apple of her eye.

It was an MGB convertible, clean white with a black ragtop and trim, the kind of car they simply don't make anymore. My mother used it as kind of a rolling knapsack; the trunk was filled with her law school textbooks, notes, outlines, along with de-icer, oil, jumper cables, and all the different odds and ends needed to keep a California car running and roaring through a New England winter.

The thing could go. Some of my strongest memories of childhood involve the front seat of that car, a bunch of brown paper grocery bags stacked on my lap because the "back seat" was overflowing with books, watching my mother put the gearshift through its paces as she blazed up Commonwealth Avenue like something out of a Bond movie.

The man didn't know any of that. He was too busy drowning in his own life. A severe and undiagnosed manic depressive on the downward plunge of a bipolar swing, addicted to cocaine and alcohol, his experience as a student at Boston College had been transformed into a nightmare. He came down our street that night with a can of gasoline in one hand and a pack of matches in the other, looking for a place to die.

My mother never locked anything. In the years we lived in that house, we got broken into and robbed no less than four times. The funny part is that the thieves always slit a screen and came through a window or something, never realizing they could have just cruised in through the unsecured front door. My mother, even after all that, never locked the house, and never locked the car.

The man with the gasoline came down our street and found the MGB sitting in the driveway with the lock button standing at attention. He opened the door and slid into the seat. Maybe he sat there for a while, watching his breath fog the windows. Finally, he took my mother's tweed winter coat that was sitting in a ball on the shotgun seat and put it over himself like a shroud. He poured the gasoline and tossed the can onto the floor. He popped a match.

I woke that night to the sound of engines, and saw red and blue lights flashing across the ceiling. My room faced the street, so I jumped up and peered outside. The street outside my house was filled with fire trucks, police cars, and a crowd of neighbors. I saw my mother standing at the front of a knot of people, her breath pluming out into the cold air through the fist she had jammed into her mouth.

The car was in the driveway, on fire from stem to stern. Two firefighters were holding up the back end while a third put the hose to the gas tank underneath. If the thing had blown, it would have lit up the far side of our house and sent those three firemen sailing singed into the night. They got it under control in a matter of minutes, however, and soon what had been a jewel of a car sat in the driveway on melted tires, black as a lump of coal and hissing like a scalded cat. The firemen used pry bars to open the driver's side door.

The car was empty.

My mother grabbed one of the firemen by the coat and asked him something. He turned to the car and used the pry bar to open the trunk. I watched as he threw a blackened cube onto the lawn, and then another, and then another. A sodden sheaf of singed papers followed. This was all that remained of her law school textbooks, her outlines, her notes, everything she needed for the final exams that were right around the corner.

The only thing to survive the blaze was *Black's Law Dictionary,* which wound up sitting in the front entryway of the house, its melted cover smelling like barbecued benzene. By morning, there was nothing left of the car but a blackened spot in the driveway and a few scattered, twisted coins. My mother stayed in bed late that day, her eyes red and blasted from crying as she called around to classmates hoping to get permission to copy their outlines for exams.

One night about a week later, the doorbell rang. My mother opened the door to find a young man standing there in scruffy jeans and a green sweater. She asked what he wanted. He pulled a hand out of his pocket and pointed to the burned law book sitting on the entryway floor by his feet. "I'm responsible for this," he said. My mother's bright Irish blue eyes blazed as she summoned him to the kitchen table. She sat him down, wreathed him in smoke from her cigarettes, and got his story.

He told her about the depression, about the cocaine and the alcohol, about the night he tried to kill himself in her car. When that match popped alight, the gasoline had caught immediately. The burning and the smoke had terrified him, and he'd fled. Before disappearing back into the night, he had pulled the alarm box on the telephone across from our house, and waited for the sound of sirens before running away. He was at the absolute bottom, so consummately screwed up that he couldn't even get suicide right, and was there in our house to ask my mother to take him to the police.

Put yourself in her seat there in that kitchen a moment. Here he was, the guy who burned up her car and destroyed everything she needed for law school, with exams right around the corner. She'd sat through enough Criminal Law classes to know what one phone call to the cops would mean for him. Here he was, and his future was in her hands.

She thought about it for a while, and made her decision. Instead of calling the cops, she gave him the telephone number for the person in charge of Health and Human Services at Boston College, a man she'd known and worked with for years. She told the kid to call her friend at HHS, and to get himself into a program. If he quit the program before it was over, she said, she'd make sure he was prosecuted to the fullest extent of the law.

The guy who burned up my mother's car got into a program and got cleaned up. He got into therapy and gained control of his depression. After a while, he moved to Chicago, where he opened a clinic to help treat inner-city kids for drug and alcohol abuse. For all I know, his clinic is still operating. We got Christmas cards from him for a few years, and then he faded out of our lives completely.

I've been thinking a great deal about this story as the debate over the future of Social Security has raged across my television and the newspapers. In all the details about private accounts, budgets, and the bottom line, it feels as though something vital is being left out of the conversation. The missing piece is simple: It is the obligation of the citizens of this country to help their neighbors when their neighbors are in need. That obligation becomes pressing when the neighbors are old, or sick, or handicapped in some way. This we call a community.

This is a large and diverse nation, with many citizens who need assistance. In order to manage the job of providing that assistance, we pay taxes to federal and state governments, which in turn disburse those monies to those who need it. Americans have been well-trained to despise paying taxes, and cutting taxes is a guaranteed winner for a politician looking to hold on to his job. Yet it was a Republican named Oliver Wendell Holmes who said, "Taxes are the price we pay to live in a civilized society." If a civilized society means roads and schools and a national defense, surely it must also mean we take care of those among us who need our help.

A lot of politicians like to talk about how this is a Christian nation. These also happen to be the same politicians barnstorming for the end of Social Security as we've known it. The Book of Matthew has Jesus teaching his followers, "If any one would sue you and take your coat, let him have your cloak as well; and if any one forces you to go one mile, go with him two miles. Give to him who begs from you, and do not refuse him who would borrow from you." Aside from being holy writ for many, that's a pretty good plan for a civilized society.

The concept for a new Social Security system being offered by those who see this as a Christian nation involves a nebulously defined process of privatization that has to date failed completely to make sense when held up to the light of basic arithmetic. In truth, their plan has more to do with winning an argument that has been raging since the days of FDR than anything else. These politicians would like to see the federal government stripped of the ability to do much besides wage war, and leave absolutely everything else to private corporations seeking to turn a profit from the process. It is worthwhile to note that the corporations seeking to enjoy the profits from this are also the ones who pay for the politicians in question. So it goes.

It is difficult to find the Christian ethic in a movement that would turn citizens into customers, that would slam the door on those citizens who simply cannot afford a for-profit safety net. It seems loving thy neighbor and blessing the meek is only good fodder for church on Sunday, leaving the other six days of the week open to turning a profit on the backs of the poor, the sick, the old, and the lame.

This is not worthy of a nation that thinks of itself not only as great, but as good. Being good costs money, and involves sacrifice. Being good involves doing what must be done to take care of the weakest among us, rather than leaving them at the mercy of a kind of economic Darwinism that would have made Jesus vomit on his own sandals in disgust. The system as it stands needs work, but not the kind of work that has been proposed. A great nation can do better. A good nation must do better.

My mother had the life of that young man delivered into her hands, and she chose to lift him up to a higher place despite the sacrifices she was forced to accept. Each of us holds the life and well-being of our neighbors in our hands. We can choose to lift each other up, or we can shrug and decide it isn't our problem. If we are indeed a community, if we are indeed good, we can make the choice to do that lifting.

THE POLITICS
OF SHOE LEATHER

06 MARCH 2006

All politics is local.

Thomas P. "Tip" O'Neill (D-MA),
Speaker of the House

IF YOU MET Rudy Perkins on the streets of Keene NH, you would not immediately suspect that you were dealing with a shaper of momentous events. If you told him he was such a man, he'd laugh and shake his head. Perkins, with his silver-toned hair and neatly trimmed moustache, has been a horticulturist and a lawyer in his time. He is self-possessed and soft-spoken, quick to smile, and easy to talk to.

The thing is, Rudy Perkins—avowed and dedicated member of the Green Party—played a significant role in one of the great stories of the 2004 election. The thing is, if you met Rudy Perkins in Keene NH, he'd likely be shaking your hand from behind a folding table covered with political and campaign literature. Perkins has, for the last several years, been working as a dedicated political activist, and in his own small way, helped to turn the state of New Hampshire blue in 2004.

Rudy Perkins is one of the founding members of a group called New Hampshire Swing the Vote. Swing the Vote was founded in the run-up to the 2004 Presidential election. The goals of the group were neither grand nor epic in scope; their mission was not to stop the

Iraq occupation or impeach George W. Bush. They weren't looking to get involved in the national push to get John Kerry elected President. Their goal was singular and narrow, small and attainable, and entirely local.

Swing the Vote sought to flip Cheshire County, in the southwest corner of New Hampshire, to the Democrats.

"There were nearly 30,000 eligible voters in Cheshire County who didn't vote during the 2000 election," says Perkins. "Bush won the state by a margin of 7,211 votes. Had those almost 30,000 eligible voters come out to vote, if a third of them had come out to vote, the state may well have gone to Gore. Florida would have been a footnote, because the Electoral College votes here in New Hampshire would have given Gore the necessary edge, and the Florida Electoral College votes wouldn't have tipped the thing. The Supreme Court would never have gotten involved."

Analyzing these numbers, the might-have-beens became unendurable to Perkins. He decided that the next election was going to be different. It worked like this: Perkins, along with Swing the Vote steering committee members Bonnie and Leah, cobbled together a group of volunteers as the 2004 election season began to loom. They mapped out Cheshire County and parceled out areas for volunteers to work. The volunteers went out in pairs, clipboards in hand, and knocked on as many Cheshire County doors as they could manage.

This was not, however, your standard canvassing project. First of all, the volunteers were sternly instructed not to stand there and proselytize to the people they spoke to. They had a series of questions to ask, beginning with "Are you registered to vote?" before moving on to "Do you vote?" and concluding with "What issues are of most concern to you?" The basic idea was to get people talking.

"It was pretty amazing," recalls Perkins. "At first, the person who answered the door would be incredulous, like they were dealing with a salesman. But the questions we asked drew them out, and allowed them to express their opinions without interruption. These days, with the television news convincing people that what they are being told is what they already believe, there isn't a lot of political conversation happening. I got the sense that, for a lot of the people I spoke to, this was the first time they were asked what their opinions were in a long time. For some of them, I really think it was the first time."

"It is a strange thing in America," says Perkins, "that, for some reason, talking about politics is improper or impolite or rude. But people really want to talk, they want to express what they believe. I had one guy talk my ear off for twenty minutes and then follow me down the driveway after I left so he could keep telling me what he believed. It was great."

Another aspect of their work that was different was the choice of whom to canvass. There were many groups making similar efforts in New Hampshire at the time. Some spoke only to registered voters, some only to registered Democrats, some only to registered Republicans. Swing the Vote decided to talk to everyone, Democrat or Republican, registered or unregistered.

Each volunteer was given a specific goal: So many doors per day, per week, per month. They wore out the shoe leather in Troy, Alstead, Swanzey, Keene, Dublin, Jaffrey, getting people to talk about what concerned them in the upcoming election. If people weren't registered, they explained how to register. They let people know that New Hampshire allows same-day voter registration, and if they wanted to, they could go down to their polling place on election day, register right there, and vote.

It worked. On election day 2004, Cheshire County saw the largest voter turnout in recent memory. Some 6,000 unregistered voters came out, people who had not been targeted by any other group because they were not on any voter roll. They registered, and they voted. Cheshire County went blue, and for only the third time since 1948, New Hampshire was won by a Democratic Presidential candidate.

"We certainly were not alone in this," says Perkins. "MoveOn, the Sierra Club, America Coming Together and a lot of other groups did great work here. But I do believe that Swing the Vote played an important role in what happened. Kerry lost the election, sure, but not in New Hampshire. We picked a goal, stuck to the mission, and won what we needed to win."

That was the trick, Perkins will tell anyone who cares to listen. One of the great difficulties on the Left is an all-encompassing sense that so much has gone wrong, and that so much needs immediate fixing. It can become unutterably daunting to try to take in the whole forest. Rudy Perkins and the Swing the Vote crew are well aware of everything that has gone sideways in the last several years, but they chose to let the forest be. They picked a tree instead, and bent all their efforts to it.

"It was all about mission," says Perkins. "We couldn't fix everything, but we could do something about Cheshire County. It required the discipline to stick to that one thing, to avoid drifting, to do it every single day. We needed to keep our volunteers on that same disciplined path—so many doors per day, a goal that can be accomplished. And it was hard. We got more than a few doors slammed in our faces. We walked miles and miles and miles."

They picked a critical area and dug in, a small piece of the larger puzzle where they could actually affect change. They did not stop the war in Iraq, end the Washington cronyism, bring accountability back to the White House, or derail the vexing budgetary priorities of this administration and this Congress. But had the election gone the other way, Swing the Vote would have, in their own small way, done a great deal to move towards addressing all of these issues.

Swing the Vote is digging in again. The 2006 midterm elections are nine months away, but as far as Perkins is concerned, it is entirely the right time to begin the back and fill. All four of New Hampshire's Congressional representatives are Republicans, all four are stalwart supporters of the Bush administration, and two of them— Jeb Bradley in the 1st District and Charlie Bass in the 2nd District— are up for re-election in November. Rudy Perkins and the Swing the Vote crew are going to tackle Cheshire County again.

"It has been said many times about each of the last two elections," says Perkins, "that each was the most important election in our lifetime. But I do truly believe that these midterms in 2006 are the most important elections in my lifetime, perhaps the most important elections since 1864. This election could very well determine the fate and future of this country, of our rights, of everything. If the Democrats can take back Congress, or even take back one wing of Congress, everything that has been happening can be stopped."

For the record, there are sixteen Republican seats up for grabs in the House this November. Six Republican senators who are running again in November have approval ratings below 50%. Fifteen seats are needed for the Democrats to take back the House, and six seats are needed for the Democrats to take back the Senate. The anemic approval ratings for both Bush and the GOP majority in Congress suggest significant Democratic gains in November are not out of the question. At a minimum, solid gains would position the Democrats to regain control of Congress in 2008, and perhaps the White House as well.

"In every sense," says Perkins, "we are looking to emulate the victors. The GOP didn't come to control the entire government by accident. They picked their spots, small areas of critical importance, and worked them. They built what they have from the ground up, one brick at a time. It took a while and a lot of work, but you can see the results today. That's what we have to do, and that's what we are doing."

Big storms gather around small particles. The folks in Swing the Vote can tell you all about that.

CINDY'S VICTORY

15 AUGUST 2005

This thing, the wheels are coming off it.

Gen. Barry McCaffrey,
after returning from an inspection of Iraq, 12 August 2005

THEY ARE SUNBURNED and storm-lashed. They sleep in tents that sit along the muddy earth of drainage ditches by the side of the road. They have been heckled by "counter-demonstrators" who chanted "We don't care!" during a rendition of "God Bless America." They have been attacked by fire ants and hassled by local health inspectors. On Thursday morning, at about 5:30 A.M., they were blasted awake by a fourteen-car convoy of Secret Service SUVs, which roared through the camp at high speed while leaning on their horns the whole time.

They have been jolted with fear when a local resident fired his weapon into the air several times to make them go away. When the shooter, one Larry Mattlage, was asked why he was firing his gun, he said, "We're going to start doing our war and it's going to be underneath the law. We're going to do whatever it takes." It is safe to say, therefore, that their lives have been threatened.

The thing is, they've already won.

Cindy Sheehan and her ever-growing band of supporters intend to stay in those ditches outside Bush's Crawford "ranch" until he comes out to talk or until 31 August, whichever comes first. If he does not come out by the end of the month, she intends to follow him to Washington and camp out in front of the White House. She and the others have been in Texas for more than a week now, garnering more and more attention from the national and international press. Yes, they are tired. Yes, they are uncomfortable. Yes, they have already won.

The nearly 2,000 crosses, crescents, and Stars of David that make up the Arlington West cemetery, erected by the demonstrators a few days ago to represent all the fallen American soldiers in Iraq, stretch almost a mile down the country road. Bush had to drive past that on Friday when he went to his fundraising shindig at the Broken Spoke Ranch. Fifty-four crosses have been added to the cemetery since he first showed up for his vacation at the beginning of August. It takes a while to drive past them all. This man, who cannot abide hearing or seeing anything in the way of dissent or disagreement, saw those crosses whistle past his window. That is a victory.

Over the weekend, as the camp prepared for the arrival of the counter-demonstrators, a huge diesel pickup truck rumbled into camp with its nose menacingly pointed towards the tents. It sat for a while, and everyone waited to see what would happen. Ann Wright, the main organizer of camp activities, finally approached the truck and met the driver. He was a father, Wright discovered, and his son had been killed in Iraq.

He did not agree with this protest, he said, but wanted to know if his son's name was on one of the crosses in the Arlington West cemetery. Ann Wright invited the man to walk the rows of crosses and find his son's name. They found it. Ann and the man from the truck sat down in front of the cross, wrapped their arms around each other, and wept. Later, the man shared a beer with Cindy Sheehan and told her he loved her. That is a victory, one that surpasses any sort of mean politics.

For three years now, both before the invasion of Iraq began and then after it was unleashed, millions of people have marched and screamed and stomped in order to try to put a stop to this disaster. The Bush administration was not pushed off its tracks even an inch in all this time. Discussions and debates on why we are there and whether or not we should leave have been bunted aside.

Many reasons for the invasion and occupation have been put forth—weapons of mass destruction, ties to al Qaeda terrorism, the building of a democracy, Hussein was a bad man—but in the end, the debate is halted by the kind of brainless thinking that left us in Vietnam for far too long: "We are there, so we have to stay." This was the accepted wisdom.

Not anymore.

All the protests, all the articles, all the books, all the whistleblowers, all the criticism combined have not packed the kind of punch that one mother in a ditch has delivered to this administration's carefully crafted fantasy vision of what is happening in Iraq. Suddenly, Bush has been forced to go before cameras and try to explain why staying in Iraq is the only option available. Suddenly, the accepted wisdom isn't so accepted anymore. A majority of Americans, according to every available poll, agree with the lady in the ditch and not with the President.

Bush isn't doing a very good job of explaining his side of things, and his people seem unable to keep their stories straight. After the fourteen Marines from Ohio were killed in Iraq, Bush got up and stated that it would be unreasonable for him to lay down a timetable for withdrawal. Yet at the same time, his generals were bent over maps and logistics notebooks, trying to do exactly that.

The *Los Angeles Times* on Saturday took a look at the mixed messages coming from the war party. "Are the president and the Pentagon on the same page over the war in Iraq?" asked the *Times*. "That question is percolating in Washington after President Bush twice in the last 10 days tried to clarify a message sent by Defense Secretary Donald H. Rumsfeld and military leaders. After Rumsfeld and other Pentagon officials indicated their desire to shift away from discussing the struggle against terrorism as a 'war'—saying it placed too much emphasis on military solutions to terrorism—Bush repeatedly used the word 'war' in an Aug. 3 speech to conservative state legislators.

"Then," continued the *Times* article, "on Thursday, Bush dismissed as 'rumors' and 'speculation' reports that U.S. commanders were contemplating significant withdrawals of American troops from Iraq next year. His comments came after Army Gen. George W. Casey, the top U.S. military official in Iraq, and Army Lt. Gen. John R. Vines, the top ground commander, had publicly raised exactly that possibility."

Hm.

On Sunday, out of nowhere, the *Washington Post* published a page-one story titled "U.S. Lowers Sights on What Can Be Achieved in Iraq." The story stated, "The Bush administration is significantly lowering expectations of what can be achieved in Iraq, recognizing that the United States will have to settle for far less progress than originally envisioned during the transition due to end in four months. The United States no longer expects to see a model new democracy, a self-supporting oil industry or a society in which the majority of people are free from serious security or economic challenges."

The article goes on to describe how any "democracy" will have to bend itself around the laws of Islam, a fact that chucks the secular-government talking points into the round file. Iraqi women should not get their hopes up about being granted significant rights of any kind. The kicker came in the third paragraph, which quotes an unnamed U.S. official saying, "What we expected to achieve was never realistic given the timetable or what unfolded on the ground. We are in a process of absorbing the factors of the situation we're in and shedding the unreality that dominated at the beginning."

In other words, the whole thing was a Charlie Foxtrot—Marine Corps parlance for "cluster fuck," defined as a series of catastrophes that lead to total disaster—from soup to nuts. There are no weapons of mass destruction, the terrorists connected to 9/11 were not there (though there are plenty there now learning how best to kill Americans with bombs), and democracy is not to be found any-where on the menu. The hearts and flowers we were promised have not come, and are not coming. Sure, Hussein is still a bad man, but that rationale for this war is an outright laugher when compared to the cost of getting rid of him. Though Bush clings desperately to his canned lines to defend his actions, the facts speak for themselves. This whole bloody enterprise has been a colossal, expensive, murderous failure. It should never have happened.

The funny part is that Bush almost certainly could have maintained the public fantasy with one simple act. He could have jumped into his pickup truck last Saturday, when Cindy Sheehan was alone except for her sister in that ditch, and driven down to see her. He could have invited her into the shotgun seat and driven her around the neighborhood for a few minutes. He could have then gone back up to the "ranch" and told the press corps that he met with her, and that they had looked into each other's hearts. That would have been the end of it.

He did not do that. Now, his generals are at loggerheads with the public line coming from the White House about getting out of Iraq. Unnamed officials are going on the record to state that the whole plan was harebrained from the word "go," and that the entire deal sits now in the ashes of its own utterly ruined failure. Bush has to keep explaining why we have to stay, why rearranging the deck chairs on this Titanic is a noble and worthwhile process. Meanwhile, the whole world mocks him for hiding from one woman and her broken heart.

Cindy Sheehan has done this with one act of conscience. She has managed to do what no other protest or action or statement has been able to do. She has knocked the wheels right off this absurd applecart. She has called the man to account. She can hang her own "Mission Accomplished" banner above her tent in that ditch. She has already won.

Her son would be very, very proud.

"NO ONE COULD HAVE
ANTICIPATED . . ."

THE VIDEO of the meeting is gut-wrenching.

There they sit, a whole room full of hurricane experts and disaster managers, shouting down a telephone line at George W. Bush, warning him a full day ahead of time that Hurricane Katrina is a catastrophe waiting to happen. There stands Max Mayfield, Director of the National Hurricane Center, emphatically explaining that Katrina is far larger and more dangerous than Hurricane Andrew, that the levees in New Orleans are in grave danger of being over-topped, and that the loss of life could be extreme.

There sits the much-maligned FEMA Director, Michael Brown, joining in the chorus of warnings to Mr. Bush and giving every appearance of a man actually doing his job. "This is, to put it mildly, the big one," says Brown. "Everyone within FEMA is now virtually on call." Brown goes on to deliver an eerily accurate prediction of the horrors to come within the Louisiana Superdome. "I don't know what the heck we're going to do for that, and I also am concerned about that roof," says Brown. "Not to be kind of gross here, but I'm concerned about (medical and mortuary disaster team) assets and their ability to respond to a catastrophe within a catastrophe."

And there, of course, is Mr. Bush, sitting in a dim conference room while on vacation in Texas, listening to all the pleas for immediate action on the telephone. With an emphatic hand gesture, Bush promises any and all help necessary. "I want to assure the folks at the state level that we are fully prepared to not only help you during the storm," says Bush, "but we will move in whatever resources and assets we have at our disposal after the storm." After the delivery of this promise, however, Bush goes mute. No questions, no comments, no concerns. As if to foreshadow what the people of New Orleans received from their leader, Mr. Bush finishes the conference by delivering a whole lot of nothing.

That's the video, nineteen hours before the bomb struck New Orleans. It is gut-wrenching because everyone now knows what came next. The storm struck, the waters rolled in, and thousands were left to die. Days passed with no help reaching the city. Images of corpses left to rot in the streets were broadcast around the globe.

It is gut-wrenching, more than anything else because of this: Four days later, when questioned about his flaccid response to the catastrophe in Louisiana, Bush stated, "I don't think anybody anticipated the breach of the levees." Right. No one anticipated the breach of the levees except the Director of the National Hurricane Center, the Director of FEMA, and a half-dozen other experts who implored Mr. Bush to take this storm seriously a full day before the hammer dropped.

No one could have anticipated it? That has a familiar ring to it.

No one could have anticipated the failure of the levees.

No one could have anticipated the strength of the insurgency in Iraq.

No one could have anticipated that people would use airplanes as weapons against buildings.

No one could have anticipated these things . . . except all the people who did. We are forced to get into some very large numbers today to accurately assess the body count from all the things the Bush administration would have us believe no one could have anticipated.

No one could have anticipated the vigorous violence the Iraqi people would greet any invaders with, said the Bush administration, except a roomful of now-unemployed generals, a whole galaxy of military experts, several former weapons inspectors, more than a few now-silenced voices within the administration itself, and millions of average citizens who took to the streets to stop the impending disaster they easily anticipated. Add this to the "No One Could Have Anticipated" body count: nearly 2,300 American soldiers, thousands of Iraqi soldiers and police, and tens of thousands of Iraqi civilians.

No one could have anticipated that people would use airplanes as weapons against buildings, said the Bush administration. Really?

In 1993, a $150,000 study was undertaken by the Pentagon to investigate the possibility of airplanes being used as bombs. A draft document of this was circulated throughout the Pentagon, the Justice Department, and to the Federal Emergency Management Agency. In 1994, a disgruntled Federal Express employee invaded the cockpit of a DC10 with the intention of crashing it into a company building. Again in 1994, a pilot deliberately crashed a small airplane into the White House grounds, narrowly missing the building itself. Also in 1994, an Air France flight was hijacked by members of a terrorist organization called the Armed Islamic Group, who intended to crash the plane into the Eiffel Tower.

The 1993 Pentagon report was followed up in September 1999 by a report titled "The Sociology and Psychology of Terrorism." This report was prepared for the American intelligence community by the Federal Research Division, an adjunct of the Library of Congress. The report stated, "Suicide bombers belonging to Al Qaida's martyrdom battalion could crash-land an aircraft packed with high explosives into the Pentagon, the headquarters of the CIA, or the White House."

On 06 August 2001, George W. Bush received his Presidential Daily Briefing. The briefing described active plots by Osama bin Laden to attack the United States. The word "hijacking" appeared in that briefing. When he received this briefing, George W. Bush was in Texas for a month-long vacation. Again. He did nothing in response. Again.

For the love of God, even the fiction writers saw this coming.

Tom Clancy's book *Debt of Honor*, written in 1994, ends with a commercial aircraft being flown into the Capitol Building during a joint session of Congress, virtually wiping out the entire government. The famous Stephen King novella *The Running Man*, written in 1982, ends in similar fashion. "Heeling over slightly," reads the ending of the King novella, "the Lockheed struck the Games building dead on, three quarters of the way up. Its tanks were still better than a quarter full. Its speed was slightly over five hundred miles an hour. The explosion was tremendous, lighting up the night like the wrath of God, and it rained fire twenty blocks away."

Add this to the "No One Could Have Anticipated" body count: more than 3,000 people killed in the Towers, the Pentagon, and in a Pennsylvania field, in addition to thousands of Afghani civilians who found themselves collaterally damaged in our attack upon that nation.

Remember the Bush-Gore debate from what seems a thousand years ago? Bush was asked about the responsibilities of an executive in a time of emergency. He said in response, "I remember the floods that swept our state. I remember going down to Del Rio, Texas . . . That's the time when you're tested not only—it's the time to test your mettle, a time to test your heart when you see people whose lives have been turned upside down. It broke my heart to go to the flood scene in Del Rio where a fellow and his family got completely uprooted. The only thing I knew was to get aid as quickly as possible with state and federal help, and to put my arms around the man and his family and cry with them."

Thousands dead in Louisiana and the surrounding states. Thousands dead in New York, Washington, Pennsylvania, and Afghanistan. Tens of thousands dead in Iraq. Is Mr. Bush crying with them, and their families, because no one could have anticipated this?

There is, perhaps, one aspect to all this that no one could have anticipated. No one could have anticipated that the United States of America would ever be governed by a man so callow, so unconnected, so uncaring, so detached, that tens of thousands of people would die during his time in office because he just didn't give a damn.

AN OPEN LETTER
TO RICHARD COHEN

GREETINGS! I was inspired to write you after reading your missive in today's *Post* regarding all the nasty emails you have received of late. Personally, I found Colbert's performance hilarious and timely, the kind of satirical backhand so desperately needed these days. I don't begrudge you your opinion that he wasn't funny, and I agree with your belief that it wasn't your opinion on his performance that motivated such an angry response.

It wasn't. You yourself nailed the reason: "Institution after institution failed America—the presidency, Congress, and the press. They all endorsed a war to rid Iraq of what it did not have."

The fact that your Colbert commentary became the flint against this rock doesn't mean that Colbert, or your opinion of him, is to blame for the resulting firestorm. The fact is that people are angry— brain-boilingly, apoplectically, mind-bendingly so—at what has happened to this great country. I am, quite often, so angry that my hands shake. Yes, a former high school teacher from New England

---

AUTHOR'S NOTE: The following letter was written in response to an article by Richard Cohen of the *Washington Post* titled "Digital Lynch Mob" dated 08 May 2006. Cohen was aghast at the angry emails he received after arguing that Stephen Colbert's routine at the Correspondents' Dinner was not funny, and went on to flatly state that such email was evidence that "the hate is back" on the Left.

here, so filled with bile and rage that I sometimes don't recognize my face in the mirror.

You, sir, should not be asking why so many of your email friends are so angry. You should be asking why you yourself are not with them in their rage. I have admired a number of your articles over these last years, and know that you are no fool regarding our situation in Iraq and here at home. It isn't your grasp of the issues that concerns me, but the absence of outrage. Do you really care about the things you write about, or is all this merely grist for the mill that provides you a paycheck?

"I have seen this anger before," you wrote, "back in the Vietnam War era." No, sir, you have not.

You hearken back to rock-throwing days in Vietnam, and lament hatred and rage. But you do not see that those days are quaint by comparison given our current geopolitical situation. Johnson and Nixon, whatever else their faults may have been, were international-ists who understood the need for connection to the wider world. The war in Vietnam, barbaric as it was, did not inspire tens of thou-sands of Vietnamese to join martyr's brigades. It did not threaten to unleash chaos in a part of the world that holds the economic lifeblood of our whole existence. It did not threaten to shake loose nuclear weapons from quasi-rogue states like Pakistan.

You speak of the angry mob because you got slapped around via email, but your characterization of the anti-war crowd tells me you have not spent a single moment out in the streets with them. I have. I have covered dozens of protests, large and small, in cities all across this country before and after the invasion of Iraq. Millions upon mil-lions of Americans participated in these, and never once, not one time, was a rock thrown.

No violence was offered anywhere, unless it was violence offered to old ladies by riot-garbed police, as was evidenced in Portland sev-eral years ago. I have the photographs to prove it. If you want to see anger, google up the picture of a 60-year-old woman holding an anti-war sign while being placed in a hammer-lock by a riot cop. You can find it by searching for "we are not the enemy portland" on the images page.

"The hatred is back," you say, as if such hatred is beyond justification. It is interesting that you make so many allusions to Vietnam; the comparison is apt, yet not on point. This is not a situation of "Then" and "Now," but "Then" and "Again." The two issues are joined by a common theme: official malfeasance, Presidential lies, administrative fear-mongering and horrific body counts in a faraway land. The lesson of Vietnam was so searing, many believed, that it would never have to be learned again.

Why the anger? Because that lesson didn't take, at least with this crowd. Why the anger? Because millions of people are staggered by the idea that, yes Virginia, we have to go through this again. We have to watch soldiers slaughter and be slaughtered for reasons that bear no markings of truth. We have to watch the reputation of this great nation be savaged. We have to watch as our leaders lie to us with their bare faces hanging out.

Why the anger? It can be summed up in one run-on sentence: We have lost two towers in New York, a part of the Pentagon, an important American city called New Orleans, our economic solvency, our global reputation, our moral authority, our children's future, we have lost tens of thousands of American soldiers to death and grievous injury, we must endure the Abramoffs and the Cunninghams and the Libbys and the whores and the bribes and the utter corruption, we must contemplate the staggering depth of the hole we have been hurled down into, and we expect little to no help from the mainstream DC press, whose lazy go-along-to-get-along cocktail-circuit mentality allowed so much of this to happen because they failed comprehensively to do their job.

George W. Bush and his pals used September 11 against the American people, used perhaps the most horrific day in our collective history, deliberately and with intent, to foster a war of choice that has killed untold tens of thousands of human beings and basically bankrupted our country. They lied about the threat posed by

Iraq. They destroyed the career of a CIA agent who was tasked to keep an eye on Iran's nuclear ambitions, and did so to exact petty political revenge against a critic. They tortured people, and spied on American civilians.

You cannot fathom anger arising from this?

I wrote a book called *War on Iraq* in the summer of 2002. That book stated there were no weapons of mass destruction in Iraq, no al Qaeda connections in Iraq, no connections to 9/11 in Iraq, and thus no reason for the invasion of Iraq. It is now almost the summer of 2006. That book was right then, and is right now, and the millions of Americans who agree with the facts contained therein have shared these four years with me in a state of disbelief, shock, sorrow, and yes, anger. None of this had to happen, and the fact that it was allowed to happen inspires the kind of vitriol you got a taste of via email.

If you want anger, you should try reading some of the emails I get on a weekly basis. The mothers, fathers, sisters, brothers, wives, husbands, and children of American soldiers killed in Iraq write to me asking why it happened, what can be done, how this is possible. They write to me because I wrote that book, because somehow they think I have an answer to that bottomless question.

I am sorry you were so wounded by the messages you received. I wish that hadn't happened; I am personally from the more-flies-with-honey school of journalistic correspondence. But in the end, truth be told, I don't feel too badly for you. It isn't an excess of outrage that plagues this nation today, but an abject lack of it. Instead of castigating those who take an interest, who have gotten justifiably furious over all that has happened, I suggest you take a moment within yourself and ask why you don't share their feelings.

This isn't Vietnam, Mr. Cohen. This is a whole new ballgame, and the stakes are higher by orders of magnitude. It took almost ten years of Vietnam for people to reach the boiling point you are so apparently horrified by (and worthy of note, that rage may have elected Nixon, but also served to stop the killing in Southeast Asia). Should those of us who are angry today wait until 2013 to raise hell?

At a minimum, I suggest you head down to your local hardware store and buy a few sheets of 40-grit sandpaper. Apply it liberally—pardon the pun—to any and all parts of your body that may be exposed to the scary anger of the anti-war Left. Toughen up that hide of yours, and greet the coming days with a leathery mien impervious to a few angry emails.

Afterwards, you could perhaps figure out why the anger of those who see this war as a crime and this administration as a disaster is so terribly threatening to you. Anger is a gift, after all, one that inspires change. If you don't think we need a change, real change, I can only shake my head.

P.S. Another reason for the anger you have absorbed can be laid, frankly, at your own feet. There are enough of us around who can still remember your words from November of 2000: "Given the present bitterness, given the angry irresponsible charges being hurled by both camps, the nation will be in dire need of a conciliator, a likable guy who will make things better and not worse. That man is not Al Gore. That man is George W. Bush."

Locate a mirror, Mr. Cohen. Stare deep within it. Know full well that today, and tomorrow, and tomorrow, will recast all your yesterdays as having passed like a comforting dream. Your ability to remain within the safe bubble of the beltway clubhouse, drifting this way and that in some meandering, rudderless fog, has ended. Al Gore invented the internet, or so we are told, and some bright-eyed editor decided to staple your email address to the bottom of your works. Welcome to the age of electronic accountability.

THE BEST OF US

II JULY 2005

*Because we don't know when we will die, we get to think of life as
an inexhaustible well. Yet everything happens a certain number of
times, and a very small number, really. How many more times will
you remember a certain afternoon of your childhood, some afternoon that's so deeply a part of your being that you can't even
conceive of your life without it? Perhaps four or five times more.
Perhaps not even that. How many more times will you watch the
full moon rise? Perhaps twenty. And yet it all seems limitless.*

Words inscribed on the gravestone of Brandon Lee in Seattle

IT WAS July 2004, and it was a hot day for Seattle. The park was filled
with activists, organizers, and regular folks, there to hear a battery
of speakers who had come together for this stop on the Rolling
Thunder Democracy Tour. I spent a couple of hours that day in a
crowded tent with election reform activist Andy Stephenson, running a teach-in on electronic touch-screen voting machines, corporate control of the vote, and what could be done about it.

I tossed in my two cents here and there, but this was Andy's show.
He had thrown his entire life into the fight for election reform, he
had crisscrossed the country a dozen times, he had raided the offices
of public officials with camcorder in hand to ask questions and
demand answers, he had run for the office of Secretary of State in
Washington on a platform of reforming the way we run elections in
this country, and on that hot July day in Seattle, he was despondent.

As we sweltered in the tent, Andy ticked off all the problems we

173

were sure to face in the coming November Presidential election. There was no independent vetting of these voting machines, he explained, so there was no way to tell if the hardware and software within was counting things properly. There were no paper ballots involved, so recounts were a thing of the past. Votes tallied on these machines would be transferred via unsecured modem to central processing computers—which were basically PCs with Windows software—that had no security and could be easily tampered with. The companies distributing these machines and counting the votes were run by men who gave money to, and in some instances actively worked for, the Bush for President campaign.

I watched the crowd slump lower and lower into their seats as Andy rattled off the grim news. Meek hands were raised here and there. "What can we do about it?" people asked. Not much more than I've done, I could feel Andy thinking, and what I've done hasn't fixed this damned situation one bit. He squared his shoulders and replied, "Get in touch with your Secretary of State and explain the situation. Write letters to the editor. Let people know this is happening. Do what you can."

Flash forward to a cold day in January 2005. I walked the route of the Bush inauguration in Washington DC, counting the protesters and the Bush supporters who were squaring off in shouting matches on every corner. It wasn't Boston cold, but it was cold enough, the chill in the air enhanced by the overwhelming police and military presence. I made my way down to the main protest gathering point, and there in the crowd was a familiar face.

Andy Stephenson stood off to the side, red hair sliding out from under a black wool cap, hands shoved deep into the pockets of his pea coat, ruddy face downcast as he watched the parade go by. We looked at each other a moment, no words available to capture the bottomless depths we felt yawning before us, and then turned to watch the show. When Bush went by in his rolling cannonball of an armored limousine, Andy and I and everyone gathered on that corner turned our backs.

Later that night we sat together with a large crew of activists in a bar that had come to be our gathering point for post-action decompression in DC. I looked over at one point and saw Andy weeping silently, shoulders shaking as all of the frustration and anger poured out of him. Everything he had warned us about in July had happened—in Ohio, in Florida, in New Mexico—and on that night he felt like an utter failure.

Several of us gathered around him to console him. I took his hand and said, "You know, Andy, it could be worse." He looked up at me and asked, "How on earth could it be worse?" I looked at him with straight-faced solemnity and said, "You could be straight." He smiled that utterly incomparable Andy Stephenson smile and laughed until he was fit to split.

That was the last time I saw him.

Andy Stephenson passed away Thursday night from complications due to pancreatic cancer. A series of strokes caused by the cancer in his bloodstream and a post-operative infection carried him to his rest. At his side were his family and Ted, his partner of nineteen years. All across the country, thousands and thousands of people who had rallied to help him heard the news, and bent their heads, and wept. He was 43 years old.

The story of Andy Stephenson's life and death carries with it all the brightness, and all the unspeakable darkness, that exists today in modern American politics. Here was a man of rare passion, an activist who poured his life into a cause, who continued fighting for this cause even after stricken with his disease, who encompassed the death of his sister and kept working, who never stopped believing that one person could make a difference.

Still, there is that darkness. It has been said that you can best know a person by knowing his enemies. In Andy's case, his enemies rank among the foulest, most despicable sub-humans ever to draw breath. A small cadre of graveyard rats endeavored to convince the world that Andy was faking his illness, that the money his friends raised to offset his medical expenses, because activists like Andy can't afford medical insurance, was actually lining his perfectly healthy pockets. They constructed websites dedicated to this premise, and they spammed dozens of blogs with their spurious claims. They deliberately interfered with the PayPal donations process organized by Andy's friends, causing a delay in payment to the hospital, which blew Andy off the surgical rotation for many critical days.

After Andy died, some of them found a thimbleful of decency within themselves and felt bad for their part in hounding a sick man into his grave. Others were not so kind. "We need to start pushing a story about how Andy Stephenson faked his own death for insurance reasons," wrote one such ghoul on the conservative forum FreeRepublic.com, where much of this horrifying behavior was organized. Another, going by the screen name AndyScam, commented on another forum where these actions were organized, "I wonder if the 'modified whipple' is what they use to treat fake cancer. lol." A few even pushed the idea that Andy had faked his death and was lounging on a beach somewhere.

The list of comments like these, the evidence of actions taken with the direct intent to harm a dying man, has been collected exhaustively. The names of the prime movers behind these attacks are known. Personally, I feel that those responsible for this should be forced to dig Andy Stephenson's grave. I believe they should be forced to spend a day with his mother, who now mourns a son after having lost a daughter. I believe they should fear the wrath of the God in Whose name they so often cloak their deeds.

That is for later, however. Andy will be remembered by his friends and family in Seattle this coming weekend. We will gather, we will sing his songs and tell his stories. We will remember the life of a man who gave of himself far more than he received, who was a patriot in the best sense of the word, whose smile could outshine the stars. We will rededicate ourselves to the causes he espoused, and we will prevail with his spirit as the wind at our backs.

Andy believed he had failed that night in January. If I could have one more chance to speak with him, I would tell him how wrong he was that night. You won, Andy. You were the best of us.

MY MORNING SONG

21 APRIL 2006

Dizzy found me last night,
Saw some kind of new light,
I woke up in a whirlwind,
Just you watch my head spin.
The spectacle that made you cry,
It's a thrill a minute plane ride,
It's overtime at ring side,
No lie . . .

The Black Crowes

THE BAR WAS MOSTLY EMPTY when I slipped onto my usual stool on Wednesday afternoon. The sun was out and a warm breeze blew through the city. Only a fool would be inside a dark saloon during such a beautiful day, I thought to myself as I took off my sunglasses. John, the bartender, shook his head at me and flashed a smile that carried just a hint of condescension; he had to be here, and was probably wondering why I would waste my day like this.

He did have a point. Spring comes to Boston about as often as honesty comes from the White House, and so far, my city was actually having one. The trees were bursting with blossoms, and the new leaves were so bright that it seemed if you touched them, your hands would come away coated in green. I even had my first near-bee experience of the season on the way there; a huge bumblebee had done a fly-by across the bridge of my nose, sounding like a truck passing on the highway.

The reason why I was there walked through the door a few minutes later dragging a huge suitcase and wearing a bright pink IMPEACH BUSH t-shirt. Cindy Sheehan had been at an anti-war event at the University of Massachusetts at Amherst the day before, all the way across the state, after coming from Austin and Crawford before that. She was flying out of Logan Airport that night to catch up with the Raging Grannies in New York on Thursday, on the eve of the huge anti-war protest that will be taking place in the city next weekend.

She had some time to kill before heading to the airport, and I was happy to offer the creature comforts afforded by my local pub. I'd brought her here last summer, while she was in town with the Out-of-Iraq tour that had come out of the Crawford protest, and she had loved the place. It was a little different on Wednesday than the last time she'd been there. The last time, it had been a Saturday night with the Red Sox in town, we had gotten to the bar just as the game had let out, and it was a zoo. This day, we had the place mostly to ourselves.

The bartender, condescending smile now gone, filled my mug with my recent favorite, the Berkshire Steel Rail. Cindy got herself a Stella Artois. Ethan, the head anti-war student organizer at U-Mass who had driven Cindy to the city from Amherst, allowed himself to get talked into a pint of the Wailing Wench, an excellent IPA. My friend Tom, an architecture student, wandered in a few minutes later and joined us.

We tried to avoid talking shop. We really did. It didn't last.

Scott McClellan was out and maybe Brit Hume or Tony Snow was going to replace him. Karl Rove got demoted, or so the story went, and was going to concentrate on keeping the GOP from getting wiped out in the midterms. Or maybe they both were being moved to the side because Patrick Fitzgerald was gearing up to indict them in his Plame investigation. Is it dangerous to have generals attack the civilian government? Or maybe those generals were firing a warning shot across the administration's bow, letting them know that if they were stupid enough to try an attack on Iran, they were going to have big trouble from the brass.

A young man wandered into the bar later in the afternoon with a friend, looking to toss back a pint or two before going to the Sox game that night. He heard Cindy and I comparing our various nightmare stories about commercial air travel; I have some good ones, but on this score, Cindy wins hands-down. He jumped in with a few good stories of his own, including one where his plane landed sideways and slid off the runway. At one point, he asked Cindy what she did that had her on airplanes so often.

"Do you remember the protest last summer down at Bush's ranch?" I asked him. "The one started by the woman who lost her son in Iraq?"

"Yeah, I remember," he said.

"Cindy Sheehan," I said, cocking a thumb at the lady next to me.

His eyes popped out of his head, and he leaped off the stool. He ran over to Cindy and wrapped her in a huge hug, and then gave her the Red Sox cap he'd been wearing. Cindy took out a pink pen and wrote, "Peace—Cindy Sheehan" on his white t-shirt. He left a little while later with the t-shirt open for all to see. Later that night, after Cindy had left, he came back from the game and told me that a bunch of people had complimented him on the shirt.

The day passed slowly and sweetly, and the beers went down smoothly. There was a lot of laughter and storytelling, and at one point we all found ourselves giggling at the absurdity of the Bush administration. Did they really have a page on their website called "Setting the Record Straight"? Who did they think they were kidding? It was all too funny. But amidst all the smiles, I saw Cindy put her head down and mutter to herself.

"Yeah, it would be funny," I heard her whisper, "if my son wasn't dead."

The time finally came for Cindy to get going to the airport. Before she left, she grabbed me by the shoulders. I really think this administration is coming apart, she told me. The lies they've told are being exposed on a daily basis. They are scared to death of the midterm elections, and we have to do everything we can to see John Conyers sitting as chairman of the House Judiciary Committee. We have such a long way yet to go, but after all this time, the work we've been doing is starting to make a difference. I hailed her a cab, piled her stuff into the trunk, and gave her a big hug goodbye.

I woke up on Thursday morning thinking about everything Cindy Sheehan has been through. She had to bury her son, Casey, and was attacked for the way she chose to mark his grave. She questioned why her son died, what the noble cause was that ended his time on Earth, and was attacked for being a traitor. She has abandoned any semblance of a normal life to travel thousands and thousands of miles in the company of strangers, for no other reason than to demand a reckoning from the people who sent her son to his death. She has been arrested and harassed, she has been the victim of death threats, and she remains undaunted.

I decided that my morning song, my morning devotion, the prayer I will offer at the start of every day, will be simple. I want Cindy Sheehan to get everything she has worked for. I want every question she has asked to be answered. I want every tear she has shed for her son to become a flood that will wash away these last five years of horror. I want her son's death, and her life, to mean something great and good for everyone, for all the people she and her son have stood for. I want the reckoning she seeks, and I believe it will come, if the rest of us display the courage and determination that has marked her passage through these dark days.

ACKNOWLEDGMENTS

A LARGE NUMBER of people played a part in the creation of this book, and I am sure I will miss a few of them.

First and foremost, I owe a debt of gratitude to Marc Ash, Scott Galindez, Brian Fitzgerald, the editors, writers, proofers, and technical crew that make up truthout.org. My work would not exist anywhere, in any form, without this organization and the people who make it work. If you don't know about this organization, you should. I flat-out guarantee that if you read truthout every day for a month, you will become the most politically knowledgeable individual in your postal district. You won't be happy about it, because a little knowledge is a caustic thing these days, but so much for all that. As the Good Doctor used to say, buy the ticket, take the ride.

A debt of thanks is owed to the owners, moderators, and community members of the web forum DemocraticUnderground.com, which is for all intents and purposes a left-wing online zoo. There is something on that forum for everyone—if you believe, for example, that George W. Bush implemented captured extraterrestrial technology to detonate the World Trade Center by way of FEMA and the North Korean Opium Tong before using remote-control devices to guide a missile into the Pentagon on 9/11, you will find allies in some of the corners of this forum—and in the long run, this is a great thing. Information is the lifeblood of this nation today, now perhaps more than ever, and DemocraticUnderground is a Mississippi River of raw data and opinion. The best part of it, for me, is the feeling you get when reading the posts that you aren't alone; there are so many people there who agree that something has gone wrong in America, and you can meet them on this forum and be comforted. You won't agree with all of them—hell, you'll probably be hard-pressed to agree with a third of them, no matter what part of the jungle you come from—but if you live in a Red State, or are surrounded by friends and family who cannot wrap their minds around what has happened here, this forum is a balm.

Many thanks to Medea Benjamin, Cindy Sheehan, Tim Carpenter, Kevin Spidel, Progressive Democrats of America, the incredible people in Rep. Conyers' office, the Veterans for Peace, the Gold Star Mothers, Military Families Speak Out, Lt. Colonel Karen Kwiatkowski, Ambassador Joseph Wilson, Ray McGovern, Andy Stephenson, all the people who gave me food and shelter while I was on the road, and every alt-media reporter and blogger who sweats blood every day to get the truth out and try to right this listing ship. These people, and many others I have not named, have shown me the definition of courage and determination.

Finally, thanks to Krissy, Hannah, Dan, Paul, Isabelle, Cara, Jim, John, Chris, Leah, Josh, Amber, Jess, Suzie, Heidi, John, Sean, Marlon, Ron, Mike, Andrew, Dave, Michelle, Anthony, Sharon, Fred, Matt, Mike, Chris, Etienne, Liz, Brendan, Steve, Carrie, Beckey, "The" Victor, Spencer, assorted barflies, and card-carrying members of the Wack-Pack, who have been my friends and have helped keep me on my feet. I'll see you in the corner.

INDEX

WILLIAM RIVERS PITT is the bestselling author of *Our Flag, Too: The Paradox of Patriotism*, *War on Iraq: What Team Bush Doesn't Want You to Know*, and *The Greatest Sedition Is Silence*. He currently serves as editorial director for Progressive Democrats of America where he writes a blog titled "We The People." Pitt continues to write for truthout.org where he was lead writer for five years. Pitt worked as press secretary for Dennis Kucinich during the 2004 presidential election, and was a high school English teacher before becoming a full-time writer and political analyst. He lives and works in Boston, Massachusetts.

OTHER BOOKS FROM POLIPOINTPRESS

CURTIS WHITE, *The Spirit of Disobedience: Resisting the Charms of Fake Politics, Mindless Consumption, and the Culture of Total Work*
Debunks the delusion that liberalism has no need for spirituality and describes a "middle way" between our red state/blue state political impasse. Features three powerful interviews with John DeGraaf, James Howard Kunstler, and Michael Ableman.
ISBN: 0-9778253-1-0, $24.00, HARD COVER

JEFF COHEN, *Cable News Confidential: My Misadventures in Corporate Media*
Offers a fast-paced romp through the three major cable news channels—Fox CNN, and MSNBC—and delivers a serious message about their failure to cover the most urgent issues of the day.
ISBN: 0-9760621-6-X, $14.95, SOFT COVER

NOMI PRINS, *Jacked: How "Conservatives" Are Picking Your Pocket—Whether You Voted For Them or Not*
Republican policies, scandals and blunders presented as they relate to the everyday contents of your wallet.
ISBN: 0-9760621-8-6, $12.00, SOFT COVER

YVONNE LATTY, *In Conflict: Iraq War Veterans Speak Out on Duty, Loss, and the Fight to Stay Alive*
Features the unheard voices, extraordinary experiences, and personal photographs of a broad mix of Iraq War veterans.
ISBN: 0-9760621-4-3 $24.00, HARD COVER

STEVEN HILL, *10 Steps to Repair American Democracy*
Identifies key problems with American democracy and proposes ten specific reforms to reinvigorate it.
ISBN: 0-9760621-5-1 $11.00, SOFT COVER

The Blue Pages: A Directory of Companies Rated by Their Politics and Practices
Helps consumers match buying decisions with their political, social and environmental values.
ISBN: 0-9760621-1-9 $9.95, SOFT COVER

JOE CONASON, *The Raw Deal: How the Bush Republicans Plan to Destroy Social Security and the Legacy of the New Deal.*
Describes the well-financed and determined effort to undo the Social Security Act and New Deal programs.
ISBN: 0-9760621-2-7 $11.00, SOFT COVER

JOHN SPERLING ET AL., *The Great Divide: Retro vs. Metro America.*
Explores differences between the so-called "red" and "blue" states and why our nation is so bitterly divided into what the authors call Retro and Metro America.
ISBN: 0-09760621-0-0 $19.95, SOFT COVER

FOR MORE INFORMATION, PLEASE VISIT
WWW.P3BOOKS.COM.